MW00799412

NYSTCE

Biology (006) Test

SECRETS

Study Guide
Your Key to Exam Success

NYSTCE Exam Review for the
New York State Teacher Certification
Examinations

Dear Future Exam Success Story:

First of all, **THANK YOU** for purchasing Mometrix study materials!

Second, congratulations! You are one of the few determined test-takers who are committed to doing whatever it takes to excel on your exam. **You have come to the right place.** We developed these study materials with one goal in mind: to deliver you the information you need in a format that's concise and easy to use.

In addition to optimizing your guide for the content of the test, we've outlined our recommended steps for breaking down the preparation process into small, attainable goals so you can make sure you stay on track.

We've also analyzed the entire test-taking process, identifying the most common pitfalls and showing how you can overcome them and be ready for any curveball the test throws you.

Standardized testing is one of the biggest obstacles on your road to success, which only increases the importance of doing well in the high-pressure, high-stakes environment of test day. Your results on this test could have a significant impact on your future, and this guide provides the information and practical advice to help you achieve your full potential on test day.

Your success is our success

We would love to hear from you! If you would like to share the story of your exam success or if you have any questions or comments in regard to our products, please contact us at **800-673-8175** or **support@mometrix.com**.

Thanks again for your business and we wish you continued success!

Sincerely,
The Mometrix Test Preparation Team

Need more help? Check out our flashcards at: http://MometrixFlashcards.com/NYSTCE

Copyright © 2017 by Mometrix Media LLC. All rights reserved.
Written and edited by the Mometrix Exam Secrets Test Prep Team
Printed in the United States of America

TABLE OF CONTENTS

Introduction

Thank you for purchasing this resource! You have made the choice to prepare yourself for a test that could have a huge impact on your future, and this guide is designed to help you be fully ready for test day. Obviously, it's important to have a solid understanding of the test material, but you also need to be prepared for the unique environment and stressors of the test, so that you can perform to the best of your abilities.

For this purpose, the first section that appears in this guide is the **Secret Keys**. We've devoted countless hours to meticulously researching what works and what doesn't, and we've boiled down our findings to the five most impactful steps you can take to improve your performance on the test. We start at the beginning with study planning and move through the preparation process, all the way to the testing strategies that will help you get the most out of what you know when you're finally sitting in front of the test.

We recommend that you start preparing for your test as far in advance as possible. However, if you've bought this guide as a last-minute study resource and only have a few days before your test, we recommend that you skip over the first two Secret Keys since they address a long-term study plan.

If you struggle with **test anxiety**, we strongly encourage you to check out our recommendations for how you can overcome it. Test anxiety is a formidable foe, but it can be beaten, and we want to make sure you have the tools you need to defeat it.

Copyright © Mometrix Media. You have been licensed one copy of this document for personal use only. Any other reproduction or redistribution is strictly prohibited. All rights reserved.

Secret Key #1 – Plan Big, Study Small

There's a lot riding on your performance. If you want to ace this test, you're going to need to keep your skills sharp and the material fresh in your mind. You need a plan that lets you review everything you need to know while still fitting in your schedule. We'll break this strategy down into three categories.

Information Organization

Start with the information you already have: the official test outline. From this, you can make a complete list of all the concepts you need to cover before the test. Organize these concepts into groups that can be studied together, and create a list of any related vocabulary you need to learn so you can brush up on any difficult terms. You'll want to keep this vocabulary list handy once you actually start studying since you may need to add to it along the way.

Time Management

Once you have your set of study concepts, decide how to spread them out over the time you have left before the test. Break your study plan into small, clear goals so you have a manageable task for each day and know exactly what you're doing. Then just focus on one small step at a time. When you manage your time this way, you don't need to spend hours at a time studying. Studying a small block of content for a short period each day helps you retain information better and avoid stressing over how much you have left to do. You can relax knowing that you have a plan to cover everything in time. In order for this strategy to be effective though, you have to start studying early and stick to your schedule. Avoid the exhaustion and futility that comes from last-minute cramming!

Study Environment

The environment you study in has a big impact on your learning. Studying in a coffee shop, while probably more enjoyable, is not likely to be as fruitful as studying in a quiet room. It's important to keep distractions to a minimum. You're only planning to study for a short block of time, so make the most of it. Don't pause to check your phone or get up to find a snack. It's also important to **avoid multitasking**. Research has consistently shown that multitasking will make your studying dramatically less effective. Your study area should also be comfortable and well-lit so you don't have the distraction of straining your eyes or sitting on an uncomfortable chair.

The time of day you study is also important. You want to be rested and alert. Don't wait until just before bedtime. Study when you'll be most likely to comprehend and remember. Even better, if you know what time of day your test will be, set that time aside for study. That way your brain will be used to working on that subject at that specific time and you'll have a better chance of recalling information.

Finally, it can be helpful to team up with others who are studying for the same test. Your actual studying should be done in as isolated an environment as possible, but the work of organizing the information and setting up the study plan can be divided up. In between study sessions, you can discuss with your teammates the concepts that you're all studying and quiz each other on the details. Just be sure that your teammates are as serious about the test as you are. If you find that your study time is being replaced with social time, you might need to find a new team.

Copyright © Mometrix Media. You have been licensed one copy of this document for personal use only. Any other reproduction or redistribution is strictly prohibited. All rights reserved.

Secret Key #2 – Make Your Studying Count

You're devoting a lot of time and effort to preparing for this test, so you want to be absolutely certain it will pay off. This means doing more than just reading the content and hoping you can remember it on test day. It's important to make every minute of study count. There are two main areas you can focus on to make your studying count:

Retention

It doesn't matter how much time you study if you can't remember the material. You need to make sure you are retaining the concepts. To check your retention of the information you're learning, try recalling it at later times with minimal prompting. Try carrying around flashcards and glance at one or two from time to time or ask a friend who's also studying for the test to quiz you.

To enhance your retention, look for ways to put the information into practice so that you can apply it rather than simply recalling it. If you're using the information in practical ways, it will be much easier to remember. Similarly, it helps to solidify a concept in your mind if you're not only reading it to yourself but also explaining it to someone else. Ask a friend to let you teach them about a concept you're a little shaky on (or speak aloud to an imaginary audience if necessary). As you try to summarize, define, give examples, and answer your friend's questions, you'll understand the concepts better and they will stay with you longer. Finally, step back for a big picture view and ask yourself how each piece of information fits with the whole subject. When you link the different concepts together and see them working together as a whole, it's easier to remember the individual components.

Finally, practice showing your work on any multi-step problems, even if you're just studying. Writing out each step you take to solve a problem will help solidify the process in your mind, and you'll be more likely to remember it during the test.

Modality

Modality simply refers to the means or method by which you study. Choosing a study modality that fits your own individual learning style is crucial. No two people learn best in exactly the same way, so it's important to know your strengths and use them to your advantage.

For example, if you learn best by visualization, focus on visualizing a concept in your mind and draw an image or a diagram. Try color-coding your notes, illustrating them, or creating symbols that will trigger your mind to recall a learned concept. If you learn best by hearing or discussing information, find a study partner who learns the same way or read aloud to yourself. Think about how to put the information in your own words. Imagine that you are giving a lecture on the topic and record yourself so you can listen to it later.

For any learning style, flashcards can be helpful. Organize the information so you can take advantage of spare moments to review. Underline key words or phrases. Use different colors for different categories. Mnemonic devices (such as creating a short list in which every item starts with the same letter) can also help with retention. Find what works best for you and use it to store the information in your mind most effectively and easily.

Copyright © Mometrix Media. You have been licensed one copy of this document for personal use only. Any other reproduction or redistribution is strictly prohibited. All rights reserved.

Secret Key #3 – Practice the Right Way

Your success on test day depends not only on how many hours you put into preparing, but also on whether you prepared the right way. It's good to check along the way to see if your studying is paying off. One of the most effective ways to do this is by taking practice tests to evaluate your progress. Practice tests are useful because they show exactly where you need to improve. Every time you take a practice test, pay special attention to these three groups of questions:

- The questions you got wrong
- The questions you had to guess on, even if you guessed right
- The questions you found difficult or slow to work through

This will show you exactly what your weak areas are, and where you need to devote more study time. Ask yourself why each of these questions gave you trouble. Was it because you didn't understand the material? Was it because you didn't remember the vocabulary? Do you need more repetitions on this type of question to build speed and confidence? Dig into those questions and figure out how you can strengthen your weak areas as you go back to review the material.

Additionally, many practice tests have a section explaining the answer choices. It can be tempting to read the explanation and think that you now have a good understanding of the concept. However, an explanation likely only covers part of the question's broader context. Even if the explanation makes sense, **go back and investigate** every concept related to the question until you're positive you have a thorough understanding.

As you go along, keep in mind that the practice test is just that: practice. Memorizing these questions and answers will not be very helpful on the actual test because it is unlikely to have any of the same exact questions. If you only know the right answers to the sample questions, you won't be prepared for the real thing. **Study the concepts** until you understand them fully, and then you'll be able to answer any question that shows up on the test.

It's important to wait on the practice tests until you're ready. If you take a test on your first day of study, you may be overwhelmed by the amount of material covered and how much you need to learn. Work up to it gradually.

On test day, you'll need to be prepared for answering questions, managing your time, and using the test-taking strategies you've learned. It's a lot to balance, like a mental marathon that will have a big impact on your future. Like training for a marathon, you'll need to start slowly and work your way up. When test day arrives, you'll be ready.

Start with the strategies you've read in the first two Secret Keys—plan your course and study in the way that works best for you. If you have time, consider using multiple study resources to get different approaches to the same concepts. It can be helpful to see difficult concepts from more than one angle. Then find a good source for practice tests. Many times, the test website will suggest potential study resources or provide sample tests.

Copyright © Mometrix Media. You have been licensed one copy of this document for personal use only. Any other reproduction or redistribution is strictly prohibited. All rights reserved.

Practice Test Strategy

When you're ready to start taking practice tests, follow this strategy:

Untimed and Open-Book Practice

Take the first test with no time constraints and with your notes and study guide handy. Take your time and focus on applying the strategies you've learned.

Timed and Open-Book Practice

Take the second practice test open-book as well, but set a timer and practice pacing yourself to finish in time.

Timed and Closed-Book Practice

Take any other practice tests as if it were test day. Set a timer and put away your study materials. Sit at a table or desk in a quiet room, imagine yourself at the testing center, and answer questions as quickly and accurately as possible.

Keep repeating timed and closed-book tests on a regular basis until you run out of practice tests or it's time for the actual test. Your mind will be ready for the schedule and stress of test day, and you'll be able to focus on recalling the material you've learned.

Copyright © Mometrix Media. You have been licensed one copy of this document for personal use only. Any other reproduction or redistribution is strictly prohibited. All rights reserved.

Secret Key #4 – Pace Yourself

Once you're fully prepared for the material on the test, your biggest challenge on test day will be managing your time. Just knowing that the clock is ticking can make you panic even if you have plenty of time left. Work on pacing yourself so you can build confidence against the time constraints of the exam. Pacing is a difficult skill to master, especially in a high-pressure environment, so **practice is vital**.

Set time expectations for your pace based on how much time is available. For example, if a section has 60 questions and the time limit is 30 minutes, you know you have to average 30 seconds or less per question in order to answer them all. Although 30 seconds is the hard limit, set 25 seconds per question as your goal, so you reserve extra time to spend on harder questions. When you budget extra time for the harder questions, you no longer have any reason to stress when those questions take longer to answer.

Don't let this time expectation distract you from working through the test at a calm, steady pace, but keep it in mind so you don't spend too much time on any one question. Recognize that taking extra time on one question you don't understand may keep you from answering two that you do understand later in the test. If your time limit for a question is up and you're still not sure of the answer, mark it and move on, and come back to it later if the time and the test format allow. If the testing format doesn't allow you to return to earlier questions, just make an educated guess; then put it out of your mind and move on.

On the easier questions, be careful not to rush. It may seem wise to hurry through them so you have more time for the challenging ones, but it's not worth missing one if you know the concept and just didn't take the time to read the question fully. Work efficiently but make sure you understand the question and have looked at all of the answer choices, since more than one may seem right at first.

Even if you're paying attention to the time, you may find yourself a little behind at some point. You should speed up to get back on track, but do so wisely. Don't panic; just take a few seconds less on each question until you're caught up. Don't guess without thinking, but do look through the answer choices and eliminate any you know are wrong. If you can get down to two choices, it is often worthwhile to guess from those. Once you've chosen an answer, move on and don't dwell on any that you skipped or had to hurry through. If a question was taking too long, chances are it was one of the harder ones, so you weren't as likely to get it right anyway.

On the other hand, if you find yourself getting ahead of schedule, it may be beneficial to slow down a little. The more quickly you work, the more likely you are to make a careless mistake that will affect your score. You've budgeted time for each question, so don't be afraid to spend that time. Practice an efficient but careful pace to get the most out of the time you have.

Copyright © Mometrix Media. You have been licensed one copy of this document for personal use only. Any other reproduction or redistribution is strictly prohibited. All rights reserved.

Secret Key #5 – Have a Plan for Guessing

When you're taking the test, you may find yourself stuck on a question. Some of the answer choices seem better than others, but you don't see the one answer choice that is obviously correct. What do you do?

The scenario described above is very common, yet most test takers have not effectively prepared for it. Developing and practicing a plan for guessing may be one of the single most effective uses of your time as you get ready for the exam.

In developing your plan for guessing, there are three questions to address:

- When should you start the guessing process?
- How should you narrow down the choices?
- Which answer should you choose?

When to Start the Guessing Process

Unless your plan for guessing is to select C every time (which, despite its merits, is not what we recommend), you need to leave yourself enough time to apply your answer elimination strategies. Since you have a limited amount of time for each question, that means that if you're going to give yourself the best shot at guessing correctly, you have to decide quickly whether or not you will guess.

Of course, the best-case scenario is that you don't have to guess at all, so first, see if you can answer the question based on your knowledge of the subject and basic reasoning skills. Focus on the key words in the question and try to jog your memory of related topics. Give yourself a chance to bring the knowledge to mind, but once you realize that you don't have (or you can't access) the knowledge you need to answer the question, it's time to start the guessing process.

It's almost always better to start the guessing process too early than too late. It only takes a few seconds to remember something and answer the question from knowledge. Carefully eliminating wrong answer choices takes longer. Plus, going through the process of eliminating answer choices can actually help jog your memory.

Summary: Start the guessing process as soon as you decide that you can't answer the question based on your knowledge.

Copyright © Mometrix Media. You have been licensed one copy of this document for personal use only. Any other reproduction or redistribution is strictly prohibited. All rights reserved.

How to Narrow Down the Choices

The next chapter in this book (**Test-Taking Strategies**) includes a wide range of strategies for how to approach questions and how to look for answer choices to eliminate. You will definitely want to read those carefully, practice them, and figure out which ones work best for you. Here though, we're going to address a mindset rather than a particular strategy.

Your chances of guessing an answer correctly depend on how many options you are choosing from.

How many choices you have	How likely you are to guess correctly
5	20%
4	25%
3	33%
2	50%
1	100%

You can see from this chart just how valuable it is to be able to eliminate incorrect answers and make an educated guess, but there are two things that many test takers do that cause them to miss out on the benefits of guessing:

- Accidentally eliminating the correct answer
- Selecting an answer based on an impression

We'll look at the first one here, and the second one in the next section.

To avoid accidentally eliminating the correct answer, we recommend a thought exercise called **the $5 challenge**. In this challenge, you only eliminate an answer choice from contention if you are willing to bet $5 on it being wrong. Why $5? Five dollars is a small but not insignificant amount of money. It's an amount you could afford to lose but wouldn't want to throw away. And while losing $5 once might not hurt too much, doing it twenty times will set you back $100. In the same way, each small decision you make—eliminating a choice here, guessing on a question there—won't by itself impact your score very much, but when you put them all together, they can make a big difference. By holding each answer choice elimination decision to a higher standard, you can reduce the risk of accidentally eliminating the correct answer.

The $5 challenge can also be applied in a positive sense: If you are willing to bet $5 that an answer choice *is* correct, go ahead and mark it as correct.

Summary: Only eliminate an answer choice if you are willing to bet $5 that it is wrong.

Copyright © Mometrix Media. You have been licensed one copy of this document for personal use only. Any other reproduction or redistribution is strictly prohibited. All rights reserved.

Which Answer to Choose

You're taking the test. You've run into a hard question and decided you'll have to guess. You've eliminated all the answer choices you're willing to bet $5 on. Now you have to pick an answer. Why do we even need to talk about this? Why can't you just pick whichever one you feel like when the time comes?

The answer to these questions is that if you don't come into the test with a plan, you'll rely on your impression to select an answer choice, and if you do that, you risk falling into a trap. The test writers know that everyone who takes their test will be guessing on some of the questions, so they intentionally write wrong answer choices to seem plausible. You still have to pick an answer though, and if the wrong answer choices are designed to look right, how can you ever be sure that you're not falling for their trap? The best solution we've found to this dilemma is to take the decision out of your hands entirely. Here is the process we recommend:

Once you've eliminated any choices that you are confident (willing to bet $5) are wrong, select the first remaining choice as your answer.

Whether you choose to select the first remaining choice, the second, or the last, the important thing is that you use some preselected standard. Using this approach guarantees that you will not be enticed into selecting an answer choice that looks right, because you are not basing your decision on how the answer choices look.

This is not meant to make you question your knowledge. Instead, it is to help you recognize the difference between your knowledge and your impressions. There's a huge difference between thinking an answer is right because of what you know, and thinking an answer is right because it looks or sounds like it should be right.

Summary: To ensure that your selection is appropriately random, make a predetermined selection from among all answer choices you have not eliminated.

Copyright © Mometrix Media. You have been licensed one copy of this document for personal use only. Any other reproduction or redistribution is strictly prohibited. All rights reserved.

Test-Taking Strategies

This section contains a list of test-taking strategies that you may find helpful as you work through the test. By taking what you know and applying logical thought, you can maximize your chances of answering any question correctly!

It is very important to realize that every question is different and every person is different: no single strategy will work on every question, and no single strategy will work for every person. That's why we've included all of them here, so you can try them out and determine which ones work best for different types of questions and which ones work best for you.

Question Strategies

Read Carefully

Read the question and answer choices carefully. Don't miss the question because you misread the terms. You have plenty of time to read each question thoroughly and make sure you understand what is being asked. Yet a happy medium must be attained, so don't waste too much time. You must read carefully, but efficiently.

Contextual Clues

Look for contextual clues. If the question includes a word you are not familiar with, look at the immediate context for some indication of what the word might mean. Contextual clues can often give you all the information you need to decipher the meaning of an unfamiliar word. Even if you can't determine the meaning, you may be able to narrow down the possibilities enough to make a solid guess at the answer to the question.

Prefixes

If you're having trouble with a word in the question or answer choices, try dissecting it. Take advantage of every clue that the word might include. Prefixes and suffixes can be a huge help. Usually they allow you to determine a basic meaning. Pre- means before, post- means after, pro - is positive, de- is negative. From prefixes and suffixes, you can get an idea of the general meaning of the word and try to put it into context.

Hedge Words

Watch out for critical hedge words, such as *likely, may, can, sometimes, often, almost, mostly, usually, generally, rarely,* and *sometimes.* Question writers insert these hedge phrases to cover every possibility. Often an answer choice will be wrong simply because it leaves no room for exception. Be on guard for answer choices that have definitive words such as *exactly* and *always.*

Switchback Words

Stay alert for *switchbacks.* These are the words and phrases frequently used to alert you to shifts in thought. The most common switchback words are *but, although,* and *however.* Others include *nevertheless, on the other hand, even though, while, in spite of, despite, regardless of.* Switchback words are important to catch because they can change the direction of the question or an answer choice.

Copyright © Mometrix Media. You have been licensed one copy of this document for personal use only. Any other reproduction or redistribution is strictly prohibited. All rights reserved.

Face Value

When in doubt, use common sense. Accept the situation in the problem at face value. Don't read too much into it. These problems will not require you to make wild assumptions. If you have to go beyond creativity and warp time or space in order to have an answer choice fit the question, then you should move on and consider the other answer choices. These are normal problems rooted in reality. The applicable relationship or explanation may not be readily apparent, but it is there for you to figure out. Use your common sense to interpret anything that isn't clear.

Answer Choice Strategies

Answer Selection

The most thorough way to pick an answer choice is to identify and eliminate wrong answers until only one is left, then confirm it is the correct answer. Sometimes an answer choice may immediately seem right, but be careful. The test writers will usually put more than one reasonable answer choice on each question, so take a second to read all of them and make sure that the other choices are not equally obvious. As long as you have time left, it is better to read every answer choice than to pick the first one that looks right without checking the others.

Answer Choice Families

An answer choice family consists of two (in rare cases, three) answer choices that are very similar in construction and cannot all be true at the same time. If you see two answer choices that are direct opposites or parallels, one of them is usually the correct answer. For instance, if one answer choice says that quantity x increases and another either says that quantity x decreases (opposite) or says that quantity y increases (parallel), then those answer choices would fall into the same family. An answer choice that doesn't match the construction of the answer choice family is more likely to be incorrect. Most questions will not have answer choice families, but when they do appear, you should be prepared to recognize them.

Eliminate Answers

Eliminate answer choices as soon as you realize they are wrong, but make sure you consider all possibilities. If you are eliminating answer choices and realize that the last one you are left with is also wrong, don't panic. Start over and consider each choice again. There may be something you missed the first time that you will realize on the second pass.

Avoid Fact Traps

Don't be distracted by an answer choice that is factually true but doesn't answer the question. You are looking for the choice that answers the question. Stay focused on what the question is asking for so you don't accidentally pick an answer that is true but incorrect. Always go back to the question and make sure the answer choice you've selected actually answers the question and is not merely a true statement.

Extreme Statements

In general, you should avoid answers that put forth extreme actions as standard practice or proclaim controversial ideas as established fact. An answer choice that states the "process should be used in certain situations, if..." is much more likely to be correct than one that states the "process should be discontinued completely." The first is a calm rational statement and doesn't even make a

- 11 -

Copyright © Mometrix Media. You have been licensed one copy of this document for personal use only. Any other reproduction or redistribution is strictly prohibited. All rights reserved.

definitive, uncompromising stance, using a hedge word *if* to provide wiggle room, whereas the second choice is a radical idea and far more extreme.

Benchmark

As you read through the answer choices and you come across one that seems to answer the question well, mentally select that answer choice. This is not your final answer, but it's the one that will help you evaluate the other answer choices. The one that you selected is your benchmark or standard for judging each of the other answer choices. Every other answer choice must be compared to your benchmark. That choice is correct until proven otherwise by another answer choice beating it. If you find a better answer, then that one becomes your new benchmark. Once you've decided that no other choice answers the question as well as your benchmark, you have your final answer.

Predict the Answer

Before you even start looking at the answer choices, it is often best to try to predict the answer. When you come up with the answer on your own, it is easier to avoid distractions and traps because you will know exactly what to look for. The right answer choice is unlikely to be word-for-word what you came up with, but it should be a close match. Even if you are confident that you have the right answer, you should still take the time to read each option before moving on.

General Strategies

Tough Questions

If you are stumped on a problem or it appears too hard or too difficult, don't waste time. Move on! Remember though, if you can quickly check for obviously incorrect answer choices, your chances of guessing correctly are greatly improved. Before you completely give up, at least try to knock out a couple of possible answers. Eliminate what you can and then guess at the remaining answer choices before moving on.

Check Your Work

Since you will probably not know every term listed and the answer to every question, it is important that you get credit for the ones that you do know. Don't miss any questions through careless mistakes. If at all possible, try to take a second to look back over your answer selection and make sure you've selected the correct answer choice and haven't made a costly careless mistake (such as marking an answer choice that you didn't mean to mark). This quick double check should more than pay for itself in caught mistakes for the time it costs.

Pace Yourself

It's easy to be overwhelmed when you're looking at a page full of questions; your mind is confused and full of random thoughts, and the clock is ticking down faster than you would like. Calm down and maintain the pace that you have set for yourself. Especially as you get down to the last few minutes of the test, don't let the small numbers on the clock make you panic. As long as you are on track by monitoring your pace, you are guaranteed to have time for each question.

Copyright © Mometrix Media. You have been licensed one copy of this document for personal use only. Any other reproduction or redistribution is strictly prohibited. All rights reserved.

Don't Rush

It is very easy to make errors when you are in a hurry. Maintaining a fast pace in answering questions is pointless if it makes you miss questions that you would have gotten right otherwise. Test writers like to include distracting information and wrong answers that seem right. Taking a little extra time to avoid careless mistakes can make all the difference in your test score. Find a pace that allows you to be confident in the answers that you select.

Keep Moving

Panicking will not help you pass the test, so do your best to stay calm and keep moving. Taking deep breaths and going through the answer elimination steps you practiced can help to break through a stress barrier and keep your pace.

Final Notes

The combination of a solid foundation of content knowledge and the confidence that comes from practicing your plan for applying that knowledge is the key to maximizing your performance on test day. As your foundation of content knowledge is built up and strengthened, you'll find that the strategies included in this chapter become more and more effective in helping you quickly sift through the distractions and traps of the test to isolate the correct answer.

Now it's time to move on to the test content chapters of this book, but be sure to keep your goal in mind. As you read, think about how you will be able to apply this information on the test. If you've already seen sample questions for the test and you have an idea of the question format and style, try to come up with questions of your own that you can answer based on what you're reading. This will give you valuable practice applying your knowledge in the same ways you can expect to on test day.

Good luck and good studying!

Copyright © Mometrix Media. You have been licensed one copy of this document for personal use only. Any other reproduction or redistribution is strictly prohibited. All rights reserved.

Copyright © Mometrix Media. You have been licensed one copy of this document for personal use only. Any other reproduction or redistribution is strictly prohibited. All rights reserved.

Foundations of Scientific Inquiry

Chemical nature of biology

All organisms are made up of matter and display the typical physical and chemical properties of matter. Every cell of an organism is composed of molecules, atoms, and ions. Chemistry is needed to explain the structure and function of all cellular processes at the molecular level. Organic chemistry involves many large and complex molecules including the biochemical compounds carbohydrates, lipids, proteins, and nucleic acids. Chemical reactions occur in the daily function of organisms even at the cellular level. Chemical reactions that are important for life include oxidation-reduction, dehydration synthesis, hydrolysis, phosphorylation, and acid-base reactions.

Use of mathematics in biology

Mathematics in becoming increasingly prevalent in modern biology especially with the use of computers for statistical programs. Mathematics is used in the studies of populations. For example, biologists study human population growth, bacteria growth, and virus growth. Populations of organisms in feeding relationships such as predator and prey are studied. Mathematics is used in classical genetics. For example, biologists use probability theory to predict offspring in genetic crosses. Mathematics is used extensively in bioinformatics. For example, biological data are extracted and analyzed using sophisticated computer programing. Mathematics is used in studies of epidemics. For example, studies concerning the spread of the flu and acquired immune deficiency syndrome (AIDS) have been performed.

Physical laws and principles governing biological systems

Biological systems are governed by the same physical laws and principles that govern the rest of the universe. For example, biological systems must obey the laws of thermodynamics. These laws govern energy and the transformations of energy. The first law of thermodynamics is the law of conservation of energy, which states that energy is neither created nor destroyed but can change forms. The energy needed for life on Earth comes from the Sun. Sunlight reaches the Earth and is transformed by green plants and cyanobacteria during photosynthesis into the chemical bonds of ATP molecules, which can be used by these organisms for energy. Consumers eat the producers or other consumers in order to obtain energy. The second law of thermodynamics states that systems tend toward more disorder or entropy and less energy. This is evident in the fact that organisms must continually acquire energy to sustain life. Energy is continuously entering the biosphere from the sun, and that energy is continuously being dissipated as stated in the second law of thermodynamics.

Observations

The two main categories of observation are quantitative and qualitative. Quantitative observations should be objective rather than subjective. Quantitative observations involve numbers and measurements. Quantitative observations can be made with instruments. Results are based on statistics and numerical analyses. Quantitative observations are used in most scientific research. Qualitative observations are typically more subjective than quantitative observations. Observing human behavior is one type of qualitative observations. Qualitative observations use the senses: sight, hearing, smell, touch, and taste. Qualitative observations are often used in the social sciences.

Copyright © Mometrix Media. You have been licensed one copy of this document for personal use only. Any other reproduction or redistribution is strictly prohibited. All rights reserved.

Hypothesis

After scientists choose a problem and make observations, they need to form a hypothesis. After studying the observations, scientists make a sensible prediction or educated guess that answers the question introduced in the problem. Hypotheses are often stated in the form an if/then statement. A good hypothesis is testable, which means that it should enable the scientist to make predictions that can then be tested. Next, the scientist designs an experiment that tests the hypothesis and predictions. A valid experiment will have several controls, one independent variable, and one dependent variable. When performing the experiment, meticulous data collection must be undertaken. Scientists should conduct as many trials as are reasonably possible.

> **Review Video: Scientific Hypothesis and Theories**
> Visit mometrix.com/academy and enter code: 918083

Variables and controls in scientific experiments

Scientific experiments involve many factors, which can be classified as either variables or controls. Variables are usually described as independent or dependent. An independent variable is the factor that is manipulated or varied during the experiment. A dependent variable is the factor that is influenced by the independent variable. This is the factor that is being measured. Controls are factors that remain unchanged or are held constant during an experiment. These factors are held constant to keep them from affecting the dependent variable when the independent variable is being varied. Therefore, controls are factors that are not being tested. Controls are used for comparison.

> **Review Video: Experimental Science**
> Visit mometrix.com/academy and enter code: 283092

Drawing scientific conclusions

After performing an experiment, scientists need to examine the data to form conclusions. Conclusions should summarize the results and state the relationship between the dependent and independent variables. Then, the scientist compares these results with the initial hypothesis. Either the experiment supports the hypothesis, or the data refute or do not support the hypothesis. Although a hypothesis can be rejected, a hypothesis is never proven true. The data cannot prove the hypothesis is true 100% of the time. They can only support the hypothesis.

> **Review Video: Fact, Conclusion, Cause and Effect, Model, and Scientific Law**
> Visit mometrix.com/academy and enter code: 534217

Testable nature of hypotheses

A valid hypothesis must be testable. A testable hypothesis should generate predictions of outcomes and tests or experiments that can be formed from those predictions. A testable hypothesis should limit variables. From a testable hypothesis, it should be clear which variable is the independent variable and which one is the dependent variable. From a testable hypothesis, an experiment that varies the independent variable while monitoring or measuring the dependent variable should be able to be constructed. If the variables cannot be measured, then a valid experiment is not possible,

Copyright © Mometrix Media. You have been licensed one copy of this document for personal use only. Any other reproduction or redistribution is strictly prohibited. All rights reserved.

and the hypothesis is not valid. If the other factors associated with the experiments cannot be controlled, then the hypothesis is not valid.

Review Video: **The Scientific Method**
Visit mometrix.com/academy and enter code: 191386

Formulation of theories based on accumulated data

Scientific theories can be formulated based on the accumulated data from the testing of valid hypotheses. Whereas hypotheses are narrow, theories are much broader. A scientific theory can summarize several related hypotheses that have been supported by repeated tests as shown in the accumulated data. As data accumulate in support of these hypotheses, a theory is developed to summarize them. The theory is then accepted as a valid explanation or model of the phenomenon examined by the testing. Theories remain valid unless they are disproved. Theories may be modified as more information and newer technologies become available. Occasionally, theories become scientific laws.

Durability of scientific laws

The very nature of scientific laws makes them durable. Scientific laws are based on observations from repeated experiments. Scientific laws are concise statements that describe some phenomenon or relationship in the world. Unlike scientific theories, scientific laws do not explain the phenomenon or relationship they describe. A scientific law is always valid under the same conditions and should imply a causal relationship between elements. Many scientific laws are written as mathematical equations. For example, Isaac Newton's second law of motion can simply be stated as $F = ma$, in which F is the force applied to an object, m is the mass of the object, and a is the object's acceleration. Scientific laws are rarely refuted.

Cell theory

The cell theory states that all living things are composed of cells and that cells come from preexisting cells. Cells were first observed in 1655 by Robert Hooke when he was studying thin slices of a piece of cork under his primitive microscope. Because the cork cells were dead, Hooke actually only observed the cell walls of the cork cells. Hooke was the first to use the word "cell," which comes from the Latin word *cellula*, which means small compartment. Hooke documented his observations with sketches and published his work in his book commonly called *Micrographia*.

Germ theory of disease

The germ theory of disease states that most infectious diseases are caused by germs or disease-causing microbes or pathogens. The germ theory is the foundation of microbiology and modern medicine. Pasteur studied the fermentation of wine and the spoiling of milk. He discovered that yeast caused the fermentation of wine and bacteria caused the spoiling of milk. He developed the process of pasteurization of milk that killed the harmful microbes without ruining the taste of the milk. Then he studied diseases in silkworms and was able to determine that the causes of those diseases are protozoa and bacteria. Pasteur also thought that microbes in hospitals came from preexisting microbes instead of spontaneous generation. He disproved spontaneous generation with his work with bacteria and broth. He discovered that weakened microbes could be used in vaccines or immunizations to prevent or protect against the diseases caused by those microbes. Pasteur discovered viruses in his work, developing the rabies vaccine and treatments for those already infected with the rabies virus.

Copyright © Mometrix Media. You have been licensed one copy of this document for personal use only. Any other reproduction or redistribution is strictly prohibited. All rights reserved.

Mendel's contributions to genetics

Johann Gregor Mendel is known as the father of genetics. Mendel was an Austrian monk who performed thousands of experiments involving the breeding of the common pea plant in the monastery garden. Mendel kept detailed records including seed color, pod color, seed type, flower color, and plant height for eight years and published his work in 1865. Unfortunately, his work was largely ignored until the early 1900s. Mendel's work showed that genes come in pairs and that dominant and recessive traits are inherited independently of each other. His work established the law of segregation, the law of independent assortment, and the law of dominance.

Darwin's contributions to theory of evolution

Charles Darwin's theory of evolution is the unifying concept in biology today. From 1831 to 1836, Darwin traveled as a naturalist on a five-year voyage on the *H.M.S. Beagle* around the tip of South America and to the Galápagos Islands. He studied finches, took copious amounts of meticulous notes, and collected thousands of plant and animal specimens. He collected 13 species of finches each with a unique bill for a distinct food source, which led him to believe that due to similarities between the finches, that the finches shared a common ancestor. The similarities and differences of fossils of extinct rodents and modern mammal fossils led him to believe that the mammals had changed over time. Darwin believed that these changes were the result of random genetic changes called mutations. He believed that mutations could be beneficial and eventually result in a different organism over time. In 1859, in his first book, *On the Origin of Species*, Darwin proposed that natural selection was the means by which adaptations would arise over time. He coined the term "natural selection" and said that natural selection is the mechanism of evolution. Because variety exists among individuals of a species, he stated that those individuals must compete for the same limited resources. Some would die, and others would survive. According to Darwin, evolution is a slow, gradual process. In 1871, Darwin published his second book, *Descent of Man, and Selection in Relation to Sex*, in which he discussed the evolution of man.

Contribution to genetics by Alfred Hershey and Martha Chase

Alfred Hershey and Martha Chase did a series of experiments in 1952 known as the Hershey-Chase experiments. These experiments showed that deoxyribonucleic acid (DNA), not protein, is the genetic material that transfers information for inheritance. The Hershey-Chase experiments used a bacteriophage, a virus that infects bacteria, to infect the bacteria *Escherichia coli.* The bacteriophage T2 is basically a small piece of DNA enclosed in a protein coating. The DNA contains phosphorus, and the protein coating contains sulfur. In the first set of experiments, the T2 was marked with radioactive phosphorus-32. In the second set of experiments, the T2 was marked with radioactive sulfur-35. For both sets of experiments, after the *E. coli* was infected by the T2, the *E. coli* was isolated using a centrifuge. In the first set of experiments, the radioactive isotope (P-32) was found in the *E. coli*, showing that the genetic information was transferred by the DNA. In the second set of experiments, the radioactive isotope (S-35) was not found in the *E. coli*, showing that the genetic information was not transferred by the protein as was previously thought. Hershey and Chase conducted further experiments allowing the bacteria from the first set of experiments to reproduce, and the offspring was also found to contain the radioactive isotope (P-32) further confirming that the DNA transferred the genetic material.

Contributions to the knowledge of DNA

The three-dimensional double-helix structure of the DNA molecule was formulated by James Watson and Francis Crick in 1953. But the actual discovery of DNA took place in 1869 when

Copyright © Mometrix Media. You have been licensed one copy of this document for personal use only. Any other reproduction or redistribution is strictly prohibited. All rights reserved.

Friedrich Miescher discovered DNA, which he called "nuclein" in the nuclei of human white blood cells while attempting to isolate proteins. Years later in 1919, Phoebus Levene identified the components of a nucleotide. Then in 1950, Erwin Chargaff published his discovery that DNA varies among species and states what is now known as Chargaff's rule: Adenine always combines with thymine, and cytosine always combines with guanine. In 1951, Rosalind Franklin studied the molecular structure of DNA using x-rays. Her work laid the foundation for the work that Watson and Crick did in 1953, in which they discovered the three-dimensional double-helix structure of DNA. Watson and Crick showed that the complementary bases are joined by hydrogen bonds. Franklin also studied the structure of RNA and discovered that RNA is a single-strand helix structure, not a double strand like DNA.

Historical and current kingdom systems

In 1735 Carolus Linnaeus devised a two-kingdom classification system. He placed all living things into either the *Animalia* kingdom or the *Plantae* kingdom. Fungi and algae were classified as plants. Also, Linnaeus developed the binomial nomenclature system that is still used today. In 1866, Ernst Haeckel introduced a three-kingdom classification system, adding the *Protista* kingdom to Linnaeus's animal and plant kingdoms. Bacteria were classified as protists. Cyanobacteria were still classified as plants. In 1938, Herbert Copeland introduced a four-kingdom classification system in which bacteria and cyanobacteria were moved to the *Monera* kingdom. In 1969, Robert Whittaker introduced a five-kingdom system that moved fungi from the plant kingdom to the *Fungi* kingdom. Some algae were still classified as plants. In 1977, Carl Woese introduced a six-kingdom system in which in the *Monera* kingdom was replaced with the *Eubacteria* kingdom and the *Archaebacteria* kingdom.

Domain classification system

In 1990, Carl Woese introduced his domain classification system. Domains are broader groupings above the kingdom level. This system consists of three domains- *Archaea*, *Bacteria*, and *Eukarya*. All eukaryotes such as plants, animals, fungi, and protists are classified in the *Eukarya* domain. The *Bacteria* and *Archaea* domains consist of prokaryotes. Organisms previously classified in the *Monera* kingdom are now classified into either the *Bacteria* or *Archaea* domain based on their ribosomal RNA structure. Members of the *Archaea* domain often live in extremely harsh environments.

Accuracy and precision

Accuracy is the exactness of a measurement. It expresses how close a measurement is to the actual or true value. Precision is the repeatability or the consistency of a measurement. It expresses how close measurements are to each other. For example, a sample weighs 10.0 grams, and the measured values of this sample are 8.8, 8.7, 8.8, 8.9, and 8.8 grams. These measurements are precise because they are all close to each other. However, although these measurements are precise, they are not accurate because they are not close enough to the actual value. For example, a sample weighs 200.0 grams, and the measured values of this sample are 200.1, 200.2, 199.9, 200.0, and 200.1 grams. These measurements are precise because they are close to each other, and these measurements are accurate because they are close to the actual value.

Scientific notation and significant figures

Significant figures indicate the precision of a measured value. All measurements are approximations and have uncertainty. The uncertainty in measurements is due to the accuracy of the measuring devices and the skill of the scientist performing that measurement. Measurements

Copyright © Mometrix Media. You have been licensed one copy of this document for personal use only. Any other reproduction or redistribution is strictly prohibited. All rights reserved.

are usually recorded to the first uncertain digit. The last digit is uncertain. The rules for using significant figures determine where to round the answers when doing calculations. Scientific notation is an easy way to write numbers that are extremely large or small. It is also a convenient way to correctly convey the correct number of significant figures in a measurement or calculations. The format for scientific notation is $M \times 10^n$, in which M is a number between 1 and 10 and n is a positive or negative integer. The first number (M) is the coefficient, and the second number (10^n) is the base. For numbers greater than 1, n is positive. For numbers less than 1, n is negative. When converting from scientific notation, the decimal point is moved the same number of places as the exponent. The decimal is moved to the right if the exponent is positive, and the decimal is moved to the left if the exponent is negative.

Metric units and notations for scientific measurements

Quantity	Unit Name	Symbol
Volume	Liter	L
Length	Meter	m
Time	Second	s
Amount of a substance	Mole	mol
Mass	Kilogram	kg
Absolute temperature	Kelvin	K
Force	Newton	N
Energy	Joule	J
Pressure	Pascal	Pa
Electric current	Ampere	A
Frequency	Hertz	Hz

Unit conversions

A convenient way to perform unit conversions is dimensional analysis. In this method, conversion unit factors are used to obtain the needed unit. For example, because 1 kilogram is equal to 1,000 grams, and 1 gram equals 1,000 milligrams, the possible conversion factors are $\left(\frac{1\ kg}{1,000\ g}\right)$ and $\left(\frac{1\ g}{1,000\ mg}\right)$. The reciprocals of these factors may also be used. To convert 2,800 mg to kg, multiply $(2,800\ mg)\left(\frac{1\ g}{1,000\ mg}\right)\left(\frac{1\ kg}{1,000\ g}\right) = 2.8 \times 10^{-3}$ kg. To convert 3,900 kg to mg, multiply $(3,900\ kg)\left(\frac{1,000\ g}{kg}\right)\left(\frac{1,000\ mg}{g}\right) = 3.9 \times 10^9$ mg.

Linear and logarithmic scales

On a linear scale, when moving from one data point to the next, the change in output is based on the difference between the two values or addition. On a logarithmic scale, the change in output is based on the ratio between the two values or multiplication. With a logarithmic scale, the value of the logarithm of a quantity is used instead of the quantity itself. Logarithmic scales cover a much broader range of values than for linear scales. For example, on a linear scale, a change from 1 to 2 could be the same as the increase from 10 to 20. But on a logarithmic scale, a change from 1 to 2 could be the same as the increase from 10 to 100. In this example, 10 was added for each increment of the linear scale, but 10 was multiplied for each increment of the logarithmic scale. One example of a logarithmic scale is the pH scale. For each increase in 1 in the value of pH, the concentration of hydronium ions increases by a factor of 10.

Copyright © Mometrix Media. You have been licensed one copy of this document for personal use only. Any other reproduction or redistribution is strictly prohibited. All rights reserved.

Identifying patterns and trends in data

Trends and patterns in data can be often be seen when reading tables, graphs, and charts by recognizing correlations between the data for the independent and dependent variables. If both sets of data increase or decrease together, then the correlation is positive. If one set of data increases and the other set of data decreases, then the correlation is negative. Often, data are represented in scatter plots, in which correlations are more readily seen. Correlations can be linear or curvilinear. Lines of best fit can be drawn for linear correlation and used to make predictions.

Graphs and charts

Pie charts are best used when comparing parts to the whole. For example, a pie chart could be used to show the components of blood and their respective percentages. Line graphs are best used when showing small or large changes over time. For example, a line chart could be used to record the weekly rainfall of a region. Bar graphs can be used to compare groups or track large changes over time. For example, a bar graph could be used to compare the average plant height of three groups of plants used in an experiment. Scatter plots are used to determine if there is a correlation between two sets of data. For example, hours of sleep could be plotted against waking blood pressure to determine a possible correlation.

Types of errors

Random errors, systematic errors, and personal errors are three types of error. Random errors are unpredictable because they are from unknown causes and cannot be eliminated. Systematic errors arise from faulty equipment or faulty procedures. Although they are difficult to detect, they may be eliminated. Personal errors are human error such as the improper use of equipment or incorrectly following a procedure. Personal errors can be eliminated or at least minimized by proper training. To calculate percent error, subtract the theoretical value from the experimental value and then divide by the theoretical value. Finally, multiply by 100 and add the percent sign.

$$\text{Percent error} = \frac{\text{experimental value} - \text{theoretical value}}{\text{theoretical value}} \times 100\%.$$

> **Review Video: Identification of Experimental Problem and Design**
> Visit mometrix.com/academy and enter code: 653245
>
> **Review Video: Identifying Controls in a Research Summary**
> Visit mometrix.com/academy and enter code: 911077

Use of graphs to identify correlations and make predictions

In order to more easily draw conclusions and make predictions, data can first be graphed. Next, the scientist looks for patterns and trends in the data to identify correlations between the independent variable and the dependent variable. Then, the scientist checks to determine if the trends and correlations observed from experimentation support or reject the hypothesis. The conclusion should state whether or not the trends in the data support the hypothesis. Predictions can often be made if the data support the hypothesis. If the data have a linear correlation, a line of best fit enables the scientist to make predictions.

Copyright © Mometrix Media. You have been licensed one copy of this document for personal use only. Any other reproduction or redistribution is strictly prohibited. All rights reserved.

Models

Models are visual representations or replicas of natural phenomena such as objects or processes that are based on scientific evidence. Models can be used to make predictions. Models help scientists explain natural phenomena that are difficult to understand. Models usually have specific limits. Models usually make approximations when describing natural phenomena. Models should be as simple as possible while still maintaining their accuracy. Many models cannot incorporate all the details of the phenomena being studied due to the complexity of the phenomena. Models have to be simple enough to use to make predictions. Models should make visualizing a process easier, not more difficult, but simplicity may be sacrificed at the expense of accuracy.

Population models

Ecologists use population models to study the populations in an ecosystem and their interactions of populations with the environment. Population models are mathematical models that are designed to study population dynamics. Ecologists can model the growth of a population. For example, models can be designed to describe increases, decreases, or fluctuations in the size of populations due to births, deaths, and migrations. Ecologists can model the interactions of populations with other populations. For example, models of the interactions between predator and prey describe the fluctuating cycles associated with these relationships. Models can also include other factors such as diseases and limiting resources.

Gel electrophoresis

Gel electrophoresis is a technique used to separate macromolecules such as nucleic acids and proteins. Fragments of DNA and RNA are separated according to length. Proteins are separated according to length and charge. The technique is relatively simple. For example, to separate DNA strands, a solution containing the DNA strand is placed in a gel. When an electric current is passed through the gel, the DNA strands migrate from the negative end of the container to the positive end due to their negative charge because of their phosphate ions. Shorter DNA strands migrate faster than the longer DNA strands. This results in a series of bands. Each band contains DNA strands of a specific length. A DNA standard is placed in the gel to provide a reference to determine the strand length. Lengths are measured in base pairs (bps).

Microscopy

Microscopy is used in microbiology. Bacteria, viruses, cell components, and molecules are too small to be seen by the naked eye. Several types of microscopes are available to examine these samples. There are light microscopes, which use visible light to study samples, and electron microscopes, which use beams of electrons. The light microscope (also called the compound microscope) uses two types of lenses (ocular and objective) to magnify objects. These are typically used when studying samples at the cellular level. Basic compound light microscopes are typically used in high school biology classes. Other compound light microscopes such as the dark-field microscope, phase-contrast microscope, and the fluorescent microscope are available for more specific uses. For tiny samples, such as viruses, cell components, or individual molecules, electron microscopes can be used. Electron microscopes use beams of electrons instead of light. Because beams of electrons have shorter wavelengths, electron microscopes have greater resolution than light microscopes. Resolution is the ability of a lens to reveal two points as being distinct. The two types of electron microscopy are transmission electron microscopy (TEM) and scanning electron microscopy (SEM). SEM is a newer technology than TEM and produces three-dimensional images.

Copyright © Mometrix Media. You have been licensed one copy of this document for personal use only. Any other reproduction or redistribution is strictly prohibited. All rights reserved.

Safety and emergency procedures for science classrooms and laboratories

Laboratory safety rules should include the following. Never perform unauthorized experiments. Read all Safety Data Sheets (SDSs) before each lab. Always pour acids into water. Avoid skin contact with chemicals. If chemicals come in contact with skin or eyes, immediately flush the contacted area with water. Never use a carbon dioxide fire extinguisher on a person—use a fire blanket. Wear appropriate apparel in the laboratory including safety goggles, aprons, and gloves when necessary. Rules for behavior include the following. No horseplay. No eating, drinking, or chewing gum. Always wash your hands when done in the laboratory. In addition to the above rules, these standard emergency procedures should be followed. Notify the instructor in case of an emergency. Be aware of fire evacuation routes and the locations of fire blankets and fire extinguishers. In the event of a fire, pull the fire alarm. In cases of ingestion of chemicals, call a poison control center.

Ethical concerns of embryonic stem cells for research

Research involving the use of embryonic stem cells offers hope for genetically related health issues. However, ethical issues are seriously debated. New therapies could be developed using embryonic stem cells that would greatly alleviate suffering for many people. However, that benefit comes at the cost of human embryos. Proponents of embryonic stem cell research argue that an early embryo is not yet a person because the embryo cannot survive without being implanted in the uterus. Some believe that the embryo should have no moral status and that fertilized eggs should be treated as the property of the parents who should have the right to donate that property to research. Opponents of embryonic stem cell research argue that the embryo is a human life at fertilization and should have full moral status at fertilization, and that a human embryo is a human being. Opponents argue that judgments determining when an embryo is viable or when an embryo is fully human cannot be made. Some opponents of stem cell research do not believe that the fertilized egg is a human being, but they still argue that by removing the stem cells from the early embryo, the embryo is prevented from becoming a human being. They argue that embryonic stem cell research destroys potential life.

Ethical and societal concerns regarding genetically modified food

Genetically modified (GM) foods are transgenic crops that have had their genes altered by technology. For example, herbicide-tolerant soybeans and insect-resistant corn have been grown for years in the United States. Several issues have been raised concerning GM foods. Some people do not want to go against Mother Nature. Even scientists may feel that because the genes in organisms have evolved over millions of years that man should not interfere. Others would argue that man has been selectively breeding plants and animals for hundreds of years, and genetic modification is just an extension of that concept. Scientists are concerned about introducing new allergens into the food supply. For example, if a gene from a peanut plant is introduced into a soybean plant, there may be a potential for allergic reactions. Proteins from microorganisms may have never been tested as allergens. Many are concerned that the genetic modifications will not be contained. Pollen from fields of genetically modified crops may be carried by insects or wind to other fields. In some cases, traits such as herbicide resistance might pass from the cultivated plants to the wild populations of those plants. Insect-resistant plants may harm insects other than those that were being targeted. For example, studies show that pollinators such as the monarch butterfly may be harmed from GM corn.

- 23 -

Copyright © Mometrix Media. You have been licensed one copy of this document for personal use only. Any other reproduction or redistribution is strictly prohibited. All rights reserved.

Ethical concerns regarding human cloning and animal cloning

Many issues are raised with the topic of human cloning and animal cloning. Disagreements arise over who would be allowed to produce human clones. Many are concerned about how clones would integrate into families and societies. Some believe that human cloning for procreation purposes should be regulated based on motivation. For example, individuals interested in raising a genetically-related child should be granted approval, but those seeking immortality or viewing cloning as a novelty should be denied. Many believe that mandatory counseling and a waiting period should be enforced. Others argue that individuals do not have a right to a genetically-related child, that cloning is not safe, and that cloning is not medically necessary. Proponents argue that cloning is needed to generate tissues and whole organs that eliminate the need for immunosuppressive drugs. Cloned tissues and organs could be used to counter the effects of aging. Others fear that this will lead to the generation of humans solely for the purpose of harvesting tissues and organs. Animal rights activists are opposed to the cloning of animals. Animals are being cloned in laboratories and in livestock production. Activists argue that many cloned animals suffer from defects before they die. Some believe that animals have moral rights and should be treated with the same ethical consideration given to humans.

Societal concerns about genetic testing

Society has not fully embraced genetic testing. Many people do not consider genetic testing to be a medical test. Many feel pressure from other family members who do not want the family genes revealed. Some do not want to know of potential health problems they may face later in life. Many are concerned about the psychological impact and stigma associated with carrying gene mutations. Many fear genetic discrimination from employers if they or a near relative carries a gene for a serious health issue. They fear not being hired, losing a job, or being denied promotions. Many fear discrimination from health insurers or being denied government services. Some fear being denied educational opportunities. Many are concerned about privacy and confidentiality. For example, who owns an individual's genetic information and who has access to that information? Should courts and schools have access to that information? Genetic testing also raises philosophical issues. Do genes determine behavior? If so, then are people responsible for their behavior? Many are completely unaware of the Genetic Information Nondiscrimination Act of 2008, which is a federal law that protects Americans from discrimination due to differences in their DNA.

Copyright © Mometrix Media. You have been licensed one copy of this document for personal use only. Any other reproduction or redistribution is strictly prohibited. All rights reserved.

Cell Biology and Biochemistry

Prokaryotes and eukaryotes

Sizes and metabolism

Cells of the domains of Bacteria and Archaea are prokaryotes. Bacteria cells and Archaea cells are much smaller than cells of eukaryotes. Prokaryote cells are usually only 1 to 2 micrometers in diameter, but eukaryotic cells are usually at least 10 times and possibly 100 times larger than prokaryotic cells. Eukaryotic cells are usually 10 to 100 micrometers in diameter. Most prokaryotes are unicellular organisms, although some prokaryotes live in colonies. Because of their large surface-area-to-volume ratios, prokaryotes have a very high metabolic rate. Eukaryotic cells are much larger than prokaryotic cells. Due to their larger sizes, they have a much smaller surface-area-to-volume ratio and consequently have much lower metabolic rates.

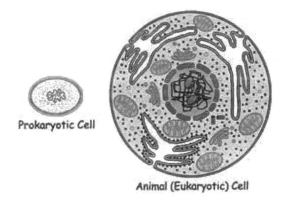

Prokaryotic Cell

Animal (Eukaryotic) Cell

Review Video: Eukaryotic and Prokaryotic
Visit mometrix.com/academy and enter code: 231438

Membrane-bound organelles

Prokaryotic cells are much simpler than eukaryotic cells. Prokaryote cells do not have a nucleus due to their small size. Their DNA is located in the center of the cell in a region referred to as a nucleoid. Eukaryote cells have a nucleus bound by a double membrane. Eukaryotic cells typically have hundreds or thousands of additional membrane-bound organelles that are independent of the cell membrane. Prokaryotic cells do not have any membrane-bound organelles that are independent of the cell membrane. Once again, this is probably due to the much larger size of the eukaryotic cells. The organelles of eukaryotes give them much higher levels of intracellular division than is possible in prokaryotic cells.

Cell walls

Not all cells have cell walls. Most prokaryotes have cell walls. The cell walls of organisms from the domain Bacteria differ from the cell walls of the organisms from the domain Archaea. Some eukaryotes, such as some fungi, some algae, and plants, have cell walls that differ from the cell walls of the Bacteria and Archaea domains. Most bacteria have cell walls outside of the plasma membrane that contains the molecule peptidoglycan. Peptidoglycan is a large polymer of amino acids and sugars. The peptidoglycan helps maintain the strength of the cell wall. Some of the Archaea cells have cell walls containing the molecule pseudopeptidoglycan, which differs in chemical structure from the peptidoglycan but basically provides the same strength to the cell wall. Some fungi cell walls contain chitin. The cell walls of diatoms, a type of yellow algae, contain silica. Plant cell walls

- 25 -

Copyright © Mometrix Media. You have been licensed one copy of this document for personal use only. Any other reproduction or redistribution is strictly prohibited. All rights reserved.

contain cellulose, and woody plants are further strengthened by lignin. Some algae also contain lignin. Animal cells do not have cell walls.

<u>Chromosome structure</u>

Prokaryote cells have DNA arranged in a circular structure that should not be referred to as a chromosome. Due to the small size of a prokaryote cell, the DNA material is simply located near the center of the cell in a region called the nucleoid. A prokaryotic cell may also contain tiny rings of DNA called plasmids. Prokaryote cells lack histone proteins, and therefore the DNA is not actually packaged into chromosomes. Prokaryotes reproduce by binary fission. The DNA in a eukaryotic cell is located in the membrane-bound nucleus. Eukaryote cells have linear chromosomes and histone proteins. During mitosis, the chromatin is tightly wound on the histone proteins and packaged as a chromosome. Eukaryotic cells may contain several large DNA molecules or chromosomes. Eukaryotes reproduce by mitosis.

Cells and organelles of plant cells and animal cells

Plant cells and animal cells both have a nucleus, cytoplasm, cell membrane, ribosomes, mitochondria, endoplasmic reticulum, Golgi apparatus, and vacuoles. Plant cells have only one or two extremely large vacuoles. Animal cells typically have several small vacuoles. Plant cells have chloroplasts for photosynthesis because plants are autotrophs. Animal cells do not have chloroplasts because they are heterotrophs. Plant cells have a rectangular shape due to the cell wall, and animal cells have more of a circular shape. Animal cells have centrioles, but only some plant cells have centrioles.

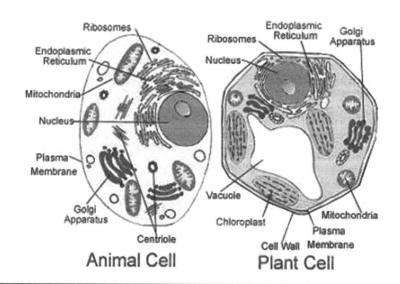

Review Video: Plant and Animal Cells
Visit mometrix.com/academy and enter code: 115568

- 26 -

Copyright © Mometrix Media. You have been licensed one copy of this document for personal use only. Any other reproduction or redistribution is strictly prohibited. All rights reserved.

Cell membranes

The cell membrane, also referred to as the plasma membrane, is a thin semipermeable membrane of lipids and proteins. The cell membrane isolates the cell from its external environment while still enabling the cell to communicate with that outside environment. It consists of a phospholipid bilayer, or double layer, with the hydrophilic ends of the outer layer facing the external environment, the inner layer facing the inside of the cell, and the hydrophobic ends facing each other. Cholesterol in the cell membrane adds stiffness and flexibility. Glycolipids help the cell to recognize other cells of the organisms. The proteins in the cell membrane help give the cells shape. Special proteins help the cell communicate with its external environment. Other proteins transport molecules across the cell membrane.

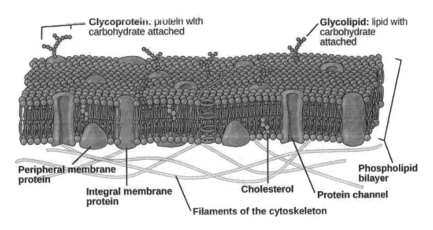

Review Video: Plasma Membrane
Visit mometrix.com/academy and enter code: 943095

Nucleus

Typically, a eukaryote has only one nucleus that takes up approximately 10% of the volume of the cell. Components of the nucleus include the nuclear envelope, nucleoplasm, chromatin, and nucleolus. The nuclear envelope is a double-layered membrane with the outer layer connected to the endoplasmic reticulum. The nucleus can communicate with the rest of the cell through several nuclear pores. The chromatin consists of deoxyribonucleic acid (DNA) and histones that are packaged into chromosomes during mitosis. The nucleolus, which is the dense central portion of

Copyright © Mometrix Media. You have been licensed one copy of this document for personal use only. Any other reproduction or redistribution is strictly prohibited. All rights reserved.

the nucleus, manufactures ribosomes. Functions of the nucleus include the storage of genetic material, production of ribosomes, and transcription of ribonucleic acid (RNA).

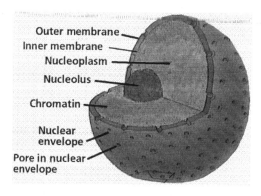

Review Video: Nucleic Acids
Visit mometrix.com/academy and enter code: 503931

Chloroplasts

Chloroplasts are large organelles that are enclosed in a double membrane. Discs called thylakoids are arranged in stacks called grana (singular, granum). The thylakoids have chlorophyll molecules on their surfaces. Stromal lamellae separate the thylakoid stacks. Sugars are formed in the stroma, which is the inner portion of the chloroplast. Chloroplasts perform photosynthesis and make food in the form of sugars for the plant. The light reaction stage of photosynthesis occurs in the grana, and the dark reaction stage of photosynthesis occurs in the stroma. Chloroplasts have their own DNA and can reproduce by fission independently.

Chloroplast

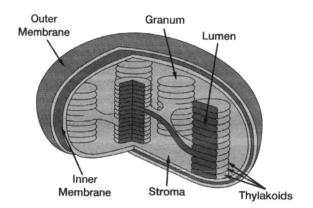

Plastids

Plastids are major organelles found in plants and algae. Because plastids can differentiate, there are many forms of plastids. Specialized plastids can store pigments, starches, fats, or proteins. Two examples of plastids are amyloplasts and chloroplasts. Amyloplasts are the plastids that store the starch formed from long chains of glucose produced during photosynthesis. Amyloplasts synthesize and store the starch granules through the polymerization of glucose. When needed, amyloplasts also convert these starch granules back into sugar. Fruits and potato tubers have large numbers of

Copyright © Mometrix Media. You have been licensed one copy of this document for personal use only. Any other reproduction or redistribution is strictly prohibited. All rights reserved.

amyloplasts. Chloroplasts can synthesize and store starch. Interestingly, amyloplasts can redifferentiate and transform into chloroplasts.

Mitochondria

Mitochondria break down sugar molecules and produce energy in the form of molecules of adenosine triphosphate (ATP). Plant and animal cells contain mitochondria. Mitochondria are enclosed in a bilayer semimembrane of phospholipids and proteins. The intermembrane space is the space between the two layers. The outer membrane has proteins called porins, which allow small molecules through. The inner membrane contains proteins that aid in the synthesis of ATP. The matrix consists of enzymes that help synthesize ATP. Mitochondria have their own DNA and can reproduce by fission independently. Mitochondria also help to maintain calcium concentrations, form blood components and hormones, and are involved in activating cell death pathways.

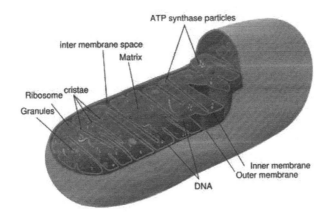

Review Video: Mitochondria
Visit mometrix.com/academy and enter code: 444287

Copyright © Mometrix Media. You have been licensed one copy of this document for personal use only. Any other reproduction or redistribution is strictly prohibited. All rights reserved.

Ribosomes

A ribosome consists of RNA and proteins. The RNA component of the ribosome is known as ribosomal RNA (rRNA). Ribosomes consist of two subunits, a large subunit and a small subunit. Few ribosomes are free in the cell. Most of the ribosomes in the cell are embedded in the rough endoplasmic reticulum located near the nucleus. Ribosomes are protein factories. Ribosomes translate the code of DNA into proteins by assembling long chains of amino acids. Messenger RNA (mRNA) is used by the ribosome to generate a specific protein sequence. Transfer RNA (tRNA) collects the needed amino acids and delivers them to the ribosome.

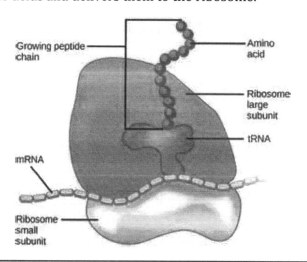

Review Video: RNA
Visit mometrix.com/academy and enter code: 888852

Golgi apparatus

The Golgi apparatus, also called the Golgi body or Golgi complex, is a stack of flattened membranes called *cisternae* that package, ship, and distribute macromolecules in shipping containers called vesicles. Most Golgi apparatuses have six to eight cisternae. Each Golgi apparatus has four regions: the cis region, the endo region, the medial region, and the trans region. Transfer vesicles from the rough endoplasmic reticulum (ER) enter at the cis region, and secretory vesicles leave the Golgi apparatus from the trans region. The Golgi apparatus directs the movement of carbohydrates, proteins, and lipids throughout the cell. Also, the Golgi apparatus helps modify proteins and lipids before they are shipped.

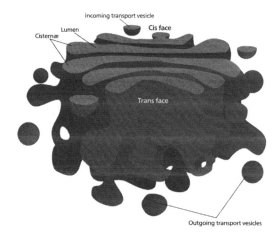

Copyright © Mometrix Media. You have been licensed one copy of this document for personal use only. Any other reproduction or redistribution is strictly prohibited. All rights reserved.

Cytoskeleton

The cytoskeleton is a scaffolding system located in the cytoplasm. The cytoskeleton consists of elongated organelles made of proteins called microtubules, microfilaments, or actin filaments and intermediate filaments. These organelles provide the shape and the needed support for the cell. They can also give cells the ability to move. These structures assist in moving the chromosomes during mitosis. Microtubules and microfilaments help transport materials throughout the cell and are the major components in cilia and flagella.

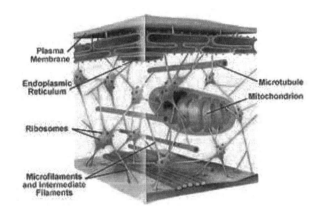

Selective permeability

The cell membrane, or plasma membrane, has selective permeability with regard to size, charge, and solubility. With regard to molecule size, the cell membrane allows only small molecules to diffuse through it. Oxygen and water molecules are small and typically can pass through the cell membrane. The charge of the ions on the cell's surface also either attracts or repels ions. Ions with like charges are repelled, and ions with opposite charges are attracted to the cell's surface. Molecules that are soluble in phospholipids can usually pass through the cell membrane. Many molecules are not able to diffuse the cell membrane, and, if needed, those molecules must be moved through by active transport and vesicles.

Active and passive transport

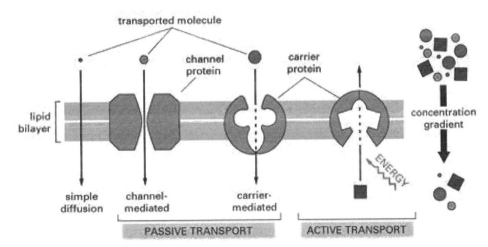

Cells can move materials in and out through the cell membrane by active and passive transport. In passive transport, the molecules diffuse across the cell membrane by osmosis. These molecules are

- 31 -

Copyright © Mometrix Media. You have been licensed one copy of this document for personal use only. Any other reproduction or redistribution is strictly prohibited. All rights reserved.

moving from a region where they have a high concentration to a region where the concentration is lower. In passive transport, the molecules move across the cell membrane without the cell expending any extra energy. Diffusion and facilitated diffusion are considered passive transport. Facilitated diffusion occurs when molecules are helped across the membrane by certain proteins called channel proteins or carrier proteins. Because facilitated diffusion is still from a region of high to low concentration, it does not require additional energy and is therefore a type of passive transport. In active transport, molecules are forcibly moved from regions where the concentration is low into a region where the concentration is higher. Carrier proteins must carry these ions and molecules, and this requires an expenditure of energy. Some ions are actively pumped across the cell membrane by proteins. Sodium ions are pumped out of cell, and potassium ions are pumped into the cell in this manner.

Water movement to maintain internal environments of cells

Cells must maintain their water balance for homeostasis. If cells have too little water, wastes and poisons can build up in the cells. If cells have too much water, the chemicals in the cells may be diluted. Water is moved in and out of cells by osmosis. Because osmosis is a type of passive transport, the cell cannot actually control this diffusion of water in and out of the cells. The amount of water that diffuses into or out of cells depends on the cell's environment. When the cell's concentration of water and dissolved solids equals that of its environment, the cells are isotonic with their environment. Cells with a lower concentration of water than their environment tend to rapidly gain water by osmosis. These cells are hypotonic with their environment. Cells with a higher concentration of water than their environment tend to rapidly lose water by osmosis. The cells are hypertonic with their environment. If cells are hypotonic or hypertonic, they must expend energy to maintain the proper water balance.

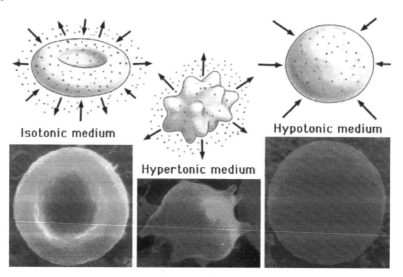

Isotonic medium

Hypertonic medium

Hypotonic medium

Use of cell surface proteins and cell communication

In order to maintain a stable internal environment, cells need to send and receive signals from the external environment. Cells have specialized surface proteins called receptors embedded in the cell membrane that allow them to communicate with this external environment. Some surface proteins are exposed to the external side of the membrane. Some surface proteins allow entry to specific materials, and others trigger chemical signals inside the cell. Because these proteins have attached carbohydrates, they are called glycoproteins. Due to the cholesterol in the cell membrane, fat-soluble materials can pass straight through the membrane, but water-soluble materials cannot

Copyright © Mometrix Media. You have been licensed one copy of this document for personal use only. Any other reproduction or redistribution is strictly prohibited. All rights reserved.

diffuse. Sodium, calcium, and potassium must use these specialized surface proteins to gain entry to the cell. These surface proteins bind to specific chemicals in the materials seeking access to the cell. This triggers a chemical signal to the interior of the cell.

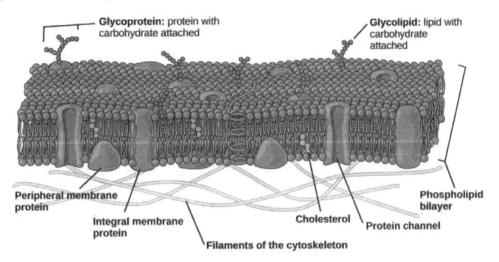

Exocytosis and endocytosis

Larger particles or groups of particles can be transported whole across the cell membrane by being packaged in a piece of cell membrane. Endocytosis is the process by which large particles are moved into the cell, and exocytosis is the process by which large molecules are moves out of the cell. Three main types of endocytosis are phagocytosis, pinocytosis, and receptor-mediated endocytosis. Phagocytosis, or "cell eating," is the process by which large solid particles are engulfed. Pinocytosis, or "cell drinking," is the process by which liquids and dissolved substances are surrounded by small sacs of cell membrane. Receptor-mediated endocytosis is the process by which molecules enter cells through receptor molecules on the cell membrane.

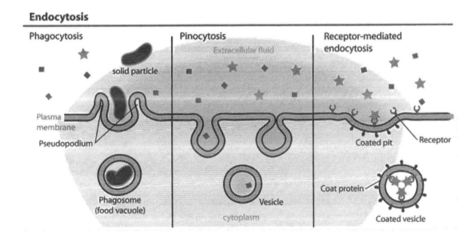

Hormone action and feedback

In order to maintain homeostasis, the endocrine system often employs negative-feedback inhibition or positive-feedback regulation. In negative-feedback inhibition, an increase in an output of a reaction to a stimulus triggers a decrease in the stimulus, which in turn causes a decrease in the original output. In positive-feedback regulation, an increase in an output leads to further increase of

- 33 -

Copyright © Mometrix Media. You have been licensed one copy of this document for personal use only. Any other reproduction or redistribution is strictly prohibited. All rights reserved.

the stimulus. An example of negative-feedback inhibition is the release of the hormones insulin and glucagon to maintain the level of glucose in the blood.

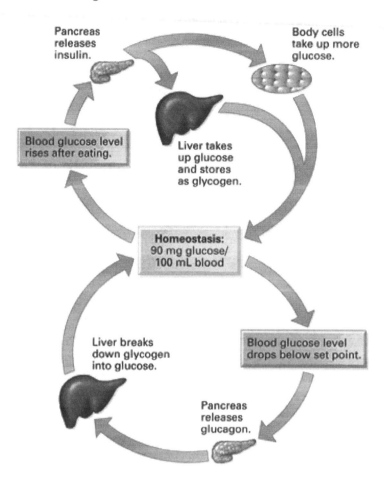

Copyright © Mometrix Media. You have been licensed one copy of this document for personal use only. Any other reproduction or redistribution is strictly prohibited. All rights reserved.

Cell cycle stages

The cell cycle consists of three stages: interphase, mitosis, and cytokinesis. Interphase is the longest stage of the cell cycle. Cells typically spend more than 90% of the cell cycle in interphase. Interphase includes two growth phases called G1 and G2. The order of interphase is the first growth cycle, GAP 1 (G1 phase), followed by the synthesis phase (S), followed by the second growth phase, GAP 2 (G2 phase). During the G1 phase of interphase, the cell increases the number of organelles by forming diploid cells. During the S phase of interphase, the DNA is replicated, and the chromosomes are doubled. During the G2 phase of interphase, the cell synthesizes needed proteins and continues to increase in size. During mitosis, the cell completes four phases: prophase, metaphase, anaphase, and telophase. During mitosis, the two sets of DNA that are arranged as the duplicated chromosomes are separated. Organelles such as chloroplasts and mitochondria also divide. During cytokinesis, the parent cell divides to form two identical daughter cells. After cytokinesis, the daughter cells begin interphase and the cell cycle starts again.

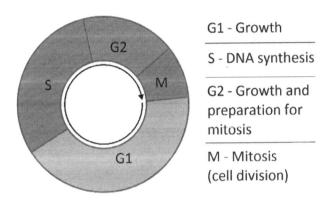

G1 - Growth

S - DNA synthesis

G2 - Growth and preparation for mitosis

M - Mitosis (cell division)

Mitosis

Mitosis is the asexual process of cell division. During mitosis, one parent cell divides into two identical daughter cells. Mitosis is used for growth, repair, and replacement of cells. Some unicellular organisms reproduce asexually by mitosis. Some multicellular organisms can reproduce by fragmentation or budding, which involves mitosis. Mitosis consists of four phases: prophase, metaphase, anaphase, and telophase. During prophase, the spindle fibers appear, and the DNA is condensed and packaged as chromosomes that become visible. The nuclear membrane breaks down, and the nucleolus disappears. During metaphase, the spindle apparatus is formed and the centromeres of the chromosomes line up on the equatorial plane. During anaphase, the centromeres divide and the two chromatids separate and are pulled toward the opposite poles of

Copyright © Mometrix Media. You have been licensed one copy of this document for personal use only. Any other reproduction or redistribution is strictly prohibited. All rights reserved.

the cell. During telophase, the spindle fibers disappear, the nuclear membrane reforms, and the DNA in the chromatids is decondensed.

MITOSIS

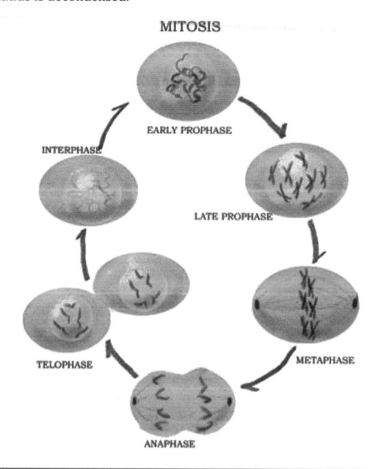

Review Video: <u>Mitosis</u>
Visit mometrix.com/academy and enter code: 849894

Copyright © Mometrix Media. You have been licensed one copy of this document for personal use only. Any other reproduction or redistribution is strictly prohibited. All rights reserved.

Cytokinesis

Cytokinesis is the dividing of the cytoplasm and cell membrane by the pinching of a cell into two new daughter cells at the end of mitosis. This occurs at the end of telophase when the actin filaments in the cytoskeleton form a contractile ring that narrows and divides the cell. In plant cells, a cell plate forms across the phragmoplast, which is the center of the spindle apparatus. In animal cells, as the contractile ring narrows, the cleavage furrow forms. Eventually, the contractile ring narrows down to the spindle apparatus joining the two cells and the cells eventually divide. Photos of the cell plate of a plant cell by transmission electron microscopy (TEM) and the cleavage furrow of an animal cell by scanning electron microscopy (SEM) are shown below.

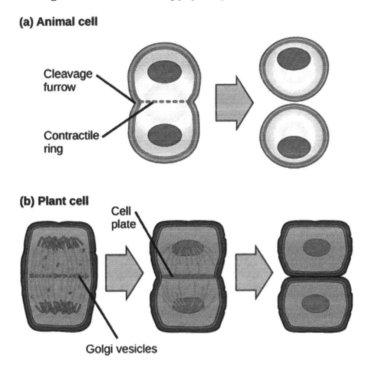

(a) Animal cell

Cleavage furrow

Contractile ring

(b) Plant cell

Cell plate

Golgi vesicles

Meiosis

Meiosis is a type of cell division in which the number of chromosomes is reduced by half. Meiosis produces gametes, or egg and sperm cells. Meiosis occurs in two successive stages, which consist of a first mitotic division followed by a second mitotic division. During meiosis I, or the first meiotic division, the cell replicates its DNA in interphase and then continues through prophase I, metaphase I, anaphase I, and telophase I. At the end of meiosis I, there are two daughter cells that have the same number of chromosomes as the parent cell. During meiosis II, the cell enters a brief interphase but does not replicate its DNA. Then, the cell continues through prophase II, metaphase II, anaphase II, and telophase II. During prophase II, the unduplicated chromosomes split. At the end

Copyright © Mometrix Media. You have been licensed one copy of this document for personal use only. Any other reproduction or redistribution is strictly prohibited. All rights reserved.

of telophase II, there are four daughter cells that have half the number of chromosomes as the parent cell.

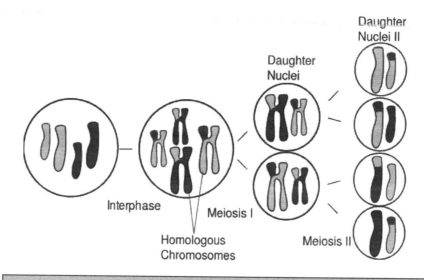

Review Video: Meiosis
Visit mometrix.com/academy and enter code: 247334

Cell cycle checkpoints

During the cell cycle, the cell goes through three checkpoints to ensure that the cell is dividing properly at each phase, that it is the appropriate time for division, and that the cell has not been damaged. The first checkpoint is at the end of the G1 phase just before the cell undergoes the S phase, or synthesis. At this checkpoint, a cell may continue with cell division, delay the division, or rest. This resting phase is called G0. In animal cells, the G1 checkpoint is called restriction. Proteins called cyclin D and cyclin E, which are dependent on enzymes cyclin-dependent kinase 4 and cyclin-dependent kinase 2 (CDK4 and CDK2), respectively, largely control this first checkpoint. The second checkpoint is at the end of the G2 phase just before the cell begins prophase during mitosis. The protein cyclin A, which is dependent on the enzyme CDK2, largely controls this checkpoint. During mitosis, the third checkpoint occurs at metaphase to check that the chromosomes are lined up

Copyright © Mometrix Media. You have been licensed one copy of this document for personal use only. Any other reproduction or redistribution is strictly prohibited. All rights reserved.

along the equatorial plane. This checkpoint is largely controlled by cyclin B, which is dependent upon the enzyme CDK1.

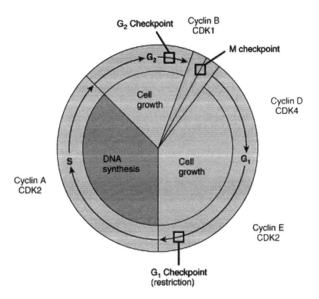

Chemical bonding properties of carbon

Carbon is considered to be the central atom of organic compounds. Carbon atoms each have four valence electrons and require four more electrons to have a stable outer shell. Due to the repulsion between the valence electrons, the bond sites are all equidistant from each other. This enables carbon to form longs chains and rings. Carbon atoms can form four single covalent bonds with other atoms. For example, methane (CH_4) consists of one carbon atom singly bonded to four separate hydrogen atoms. Carbon atoms can also form double or triple covalent bonds. For example, an oxygen atom can form a double bond with a carbon atom, and a nitrogen atom can form a triple bond with a carbon atom.

Organic and inorganic molecules

Organic molecules contain carbon and hydrogen. Because carbon can form four covalent bonds, organic molecules can be very complex structures. Organic molecules can have carbon backbones that form long chains, branched chains, or even rings. Organic compounds tend to be less soluble in water than inorganic compounds. Organic compounds include four classes: carbohydrates, lipids, proteins, and nucleic acids. Specific examples of organic compounds include sucrose, cholesterol, insulin, and DNA. Inorganic molecules do not contain carbon and hydrogen. Inorganic compounds include salts and metals. Specific examples of inorganic molecules include sodium chloride, oxygen, and carbon dioxide.

Chemical bonds

Chemical bonds are the attractive forces that bind atoms together to form molecules. Chemical bonds include covalent bonds, ionic bonds, and metallic bonds. Covalent bonds are formed from the sharing of electron pairs between two atoms in a molecule. In organic molecules, carbon atoms

- 39 -

Copyright © Mometrix Media. You have been licensed one copy of this document for personal use only. Any other reproduction or redistribution is strictly prohibited. All rights reserved.

form single, double, or triple covalent bonds. Organic compounds including proteins, carbohydrates, lipids, and nucleic acids are molecular compounds formed by covalent bonds.

Review Video: Basics of Organic Acids
Visit mometrix.com/academy and enter code: 238132

Review Video: Basics of Organic Compound Groups
Visit mometrix.com/academy and enter code: 889859

Intermolecular forces

Intermolecular forces are the attractive forces between molecules. Intermolecular forces include hydrogen bonds, London or dispersion forces, and dipole-dipole forces. Hydrogen bonds are the attractive forces between molecules containing hydrogen atoms covalently bonded to oxygen, fluorine, or nitrogen. Hydrogen bonds bind the two strands of a DNA molecule to each other. Two hydrogen bonds join each adenosine and thymine, and three hydrogen bonds join each cytosine and guanine.

ATP

Adenosine triphosphate (ATP) is the energy source for most cellular functions. Each ATP molecule is a nucleotide consisting of a central ribose sugar flanked by a purine base and a chain of three phosphate groups. The purine base is adenine, and when adenine is joined to ribose, an adenosine is formed, explaining the name adenosine triphosphate. If one phosphate is removed from the end of the molecule, adenosine diphosphate (ADP) is formed.

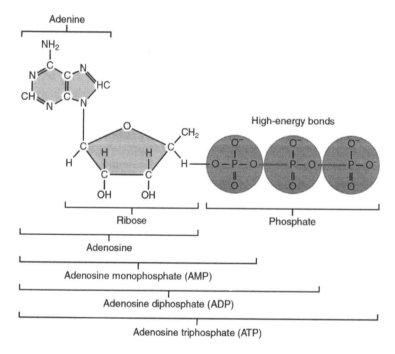

Properties of water

Water exhibits numerous properties. Water has a high surface tension due to the cohesion between water molecules from the hydrogen bonds between the molecules. The capillary action of water is also due to this cohesion, and the adhesion of water is due to its polarity. Water is an excellent

Copyright © Mometrix Media. You have been licensed one copy of this document for personal use only. Any other reproduction or redistribution is strictly prohibited. All rights reserved.

solvent due to its polarity and is considered the universal solvent. Water exists naturally as a solid, liquid, and gas. The density of water decreases as ice freezes and forms crystals in the solid phase. Water is most dense at 4°C. Water can act as an acid or base in chemical reactions. Pure water is an insulator because it has virtually no ions. Water has a high specific heat capacity due to its low molecular mass and bent molecular shape.

Biological macromolecules

Macromolecules are large molecules made up of smaller organic molecules. Four classes of macromolecules include carbohydrates, nucleic acids, proteins, and lipids. Carbohydrates, proteins, and nucleic acids are polymers that are formed when the monomers are joined together in a dehydration process. In this dehydration process, the monomers are joined by a covalent bond and a water molecule is released. The monomers in carbohydrates are simple sugars such as glucose. Polysaccharides are polymers of carbohydrates. The monomers in proteins are amino acids. The amino acids form polypeptide chains, which are folded into proteins. The monomers in nucleic acids are nucleotides. Lipids are not actually considered to be polymers. Lipids typically are classified as fats, phospholipids, or steroids.

Concentration gradients

Concentration gradients, also called diffusion gradients, are differences in the concentration or the number of molecules of solutes in a solution between two regions. A gradient can also result from an unequal distribution of ions across a cell membrane. Solutes move along a concentration gradient by random motion from the region of high concentration toward the region of low concentration in a process called diffusion. Diffusion is the movement of molecules or ions down a concentration gradient. Diffusion is the method by which oxygen, carbon dioxide, and other nonpolar molecules cross a cell membrane. The steepness of the concentration gradient affects the rate of diffusion. Passive transport makes use of concentration gradients as well as electric gradients to move substances across the cell membrane. Active transport can move a substance against its concentration gradient.

Laws of thermodynamics and Gibbs free energy

The first law of thermodynamics states that energy can neither be created nor destroyed. Energy may change forms, but the energy in a closed system is constant. The second law of thermodynamics states that systems tend toward a state of lower energy and greater disorder. This disorder is called entropy. According to the second law of thermodynamics, entropy is increasing. Gibbs free energy is the energy a system that is available or "free" to be released to perform work at a constant temperature. Organisms must be able to use energy to survive. Biological processes such as the chemical reactions involved in metabolism are governed by these laws.

Anabolic and catabolic reactions

Anabolism and catabolism are metabolic processes. Anabolism is essentially the synthesis of large molecules from monomers, whereas catabolism is the decomposition of large molecules into their component monomers. Anabolism uses energy, whereas catabolism produces energy. Anabolism typically builds and repair tissues, and catabolism typically burns stored food to produce energy. Protein synthesis, which is the polymerization of amino acids to form proteins, is an anabolic reaction. Mineralization of bones is also an anabolic process. An example of a catabolic reaction is hydrolysis, which is the decomposition of polymers into monomers that releases a water molecule and energy. Cellular respiration is a catabolic process in which typically glucose combines with oxygen to release energy in the form of adenosine triphosphate (ATP).

- 41 -

Copyright © Mometrix Media. You have been licensed one copy of this document for personal use only. Any other reproduction or redistribution is strictly prohibited. All rights reserved.

Oxidation-reduction reactions

Oxidation-reduction reactions, or redox reactions, involve the transfer of electrons from one substance to another. Reduction occurs in the substance that gains the electrons. Oxidation occurs in the substance that loses the electrons. Cellular respiration and photosynthesis are redox reactions. Cells use the energy stored in food during the redox reaction of cellular respiration. During cellular respiration, glucose molecules are oxidized and oxygen molecules are reduced. Because electrons lose energy when being transferred to oxygen, the electrons are usually first transferred to the coenzyme NAD^+, which is reduced to NADH. The NADH then releases the energy in steps to the oxygen. During photosynthesis, water molecules are split and oxidized and carbon dioxide molecules are reduced. During photosynthesis, when the water molecules are split, electrons are transferred with the hydrogen ions to the carbon dioxide molecules.

Active site structure and substrate binding

Each enzyme has a complex three-dimensional shape that is specifically designed to fit to a particular reactant, which is called the substrate. The enzyme and the substrate join temporarily forming the enzyme-substrate complex. This complex is unstable, and the chemical bonds are likely to be altered to produce a new molecule or molecules. Each enzyme can only combine with specific substrates because of this "lock-and-key" fit. Each enzyme has a designated binding site on the surface that binds to the substrate. Often, the binding site and the active site are at the same location. The enzyme and the substrate are specifically designed for each other, and they are both flexible and can bend and fold to fit into each other as they come together. This concept is referred to as the *induced fit hypothesis*.

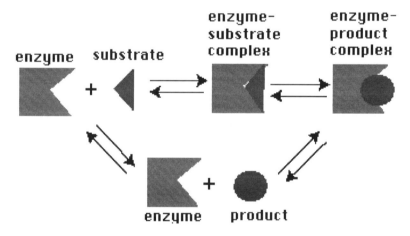

Effects of temperature, pH, and inhibitors on enzyme activity

The rate of an enzyme-controlled reaction is affected by factors such as temperature, pH, and inhibitors. According to kinetic-molecular theory, increasing the temperature increases the rate of molecular motion. Typically, increasing the temperature increases the rate of these reactions. The optimum temperature is the temperature at which the rate is the fastest and the most product is formed. Increasing the temperature above the optimum temperature actually decreases the reaction rate due to changes on the enzyme's structure that affect substrate binding. The pH also affects enzyme activity due to hydrogen ions binding to the enzyme's surface and changing the enzyme's surface shape. Because enzymes must have a specific shape for their specific substrate, enzymes have a certain pH range in which they can function. Inhibitors are molecules that attach to

Copyright © Mometrix Media. You have been licensed one copy of this document for personal use only. Any other reproduction or redistribution is strictly prohibited. All rights reserved.

the enzymes and interfere with substrate binding, thus they decreasing or even halting enzyme-controlled reactions.

Regulation of enzymes by feedback inhibition

Enzyme-controlled reactions can be regulated by feedback inhibition, or negative feedback. Feedback inhibition can be illustrated by a furnace and thermostat. The inhibitor in this system is the heat. When the furnace runs, the temperature increases. When the temperature reaches a specific level, the thermostat switches the furnace off. When the temperature decreases below a specific level, the thermostat switches the furnace back on, and the cycle begins again. In enzyme-controlled reactions, the end products of a metabolic pathway bind to the enzymes that initiate the metabolic pathway. This causes the reaction rate to decrease. The more product there is, the less product is produced. The less product there is, the more product is produced. This process of feedback inhibition enables a stable range of concentrations that are necessary for homeostasis.

> **Review Video: Enzymes**
> Visit mometrix.com/academy and enter code: 656995

Biochemical pathways

Autotrophs that use light to produce energy use photosynthesis as a biochemical pathway. In eukaryotic autotrophs photosynthesis takes place in chloroplasts. Prokaryotic autotrophs that use inorganic chemical reactions to produce energy use chemosynthesis as a biochemical pathway. Heterotrophs require food and use cellular respiration to release energy from chemical bonds in the food. All organisms use cellular respiration to release energy from stored food. Cellular respiration can be aerobic or anaerobic. Most eukaryotes use cellular respiration that takes place in the mitochondria.

Photosynthesis

Photosynthesis is a food-making process that occurs in three processes: light-capturing events, light-dependent reactions, and light-independent reactions. In light-capturing events, the thylakoids of the chloroplasts, which contain chlorophyll and accessory pigments, absorb light energy and produce excited electrons. Thylakoids also contain enzymes and electron-transport molecules. Molecules involved in this process are arranged in groups called photosystems. In light-dependent reactions, the excited electrons from the light-capturing events are moved by electron transport in a series of steps in which they are used to split water into hydrogen and oxygen ions. The oxygen is released, and the $NADP^+$ bonds with the hydrogen atoms and forms NADPH. ATP is produced from the excited elections. The light-independent reactions use this ATP, NADPH, and carbon dioxide to produce sugars.

C3 and C4 photosynthesis

Three types of photosynthesis are C3, C4, and crassulacean acid metabolism (CAM). C3 and C4 photosynthesis are named for the type of carbon molecule (three-carbon or four-carbon) that is made during the first step of the reaction. The first step of C3 photosynthesis is the formation of two three-carbon molecules (3-phosphoglycerate) from a reaction between carbon dioxide and a five carbon molecule (ribulose 1,5-bisphosphate). The first step of C4 photosynthesis is the formation of a four-carbon molecule (oxaloacetate) from a reaction between carbon dioxide and a three-carbon molecule (phosphoenolpyruvate). More than 95% of plants perform C3 photosynthesis. C4 photosynthesis can be used by plants in sunlight-intense regions because it helps conserve water.

- 43 -

Copyright © Mometrix Media. You have been licensed one copy of this document for personal use only. Any other reproduction or redistribution is strictly prohibited. All rights reserved.

Crassulacean acid metabolism

Crassulacean acid metabolism (CAM) is a form of photosynthesis adapted to dry environments. During nighttime, pores of the plant leaves (stomata) open to receive carbon dioxide, which combines with phosphoenolpyruvate (three-carbon molecule) to form malate (four-carbon molecule). Malate is stored in vacuoles. During the daytime, the stomata are closed and the malate is transported to chloroplasts, where malate is broken down into pyruvate (three-carbon molecule) and carbon dioxide. The carbon dioxide released from malate is used in photosynthesis during the daytime. One advantage of the CAM cycle is that it minimizes loss of water through the stomata during the daytime. A second advantage is that concentrating carbon dioxide in the chloroplasts in this manner increases the efficiency of the enzyme that converts carbon dioxide and ribulose 1,5-bisphosphate into two 3-phosphoglycerate molecules.

> **Review Video: Photosynthesis in Biology**
> Visit mometrix.com/academy and enter code: 402602

Aerobic respiration

Aerobic cellular respiration is a series of enzyme-controlled chemical reactions in which oxygen reacts with glucose to produce carbon dioxide and water, releasing energy in the form of adenosine triphosphate (ATP). Cellular respiration occurs in a series of three processes: glycolysis, the Krebs cycle, and the electron-transport system.

> **Review Video: Aerobic Respiration**
> Visit mometrix.com/academy and enter code: 770290

Glycolysis

Glycolysis is a series of enzyme-controlled chemical reactions that occur in the cell's cytoplasm. Each glucose molecule is split in half to produce two pyruvic acid molecules and four ATP molecules and two NADH molecules. Because two ATP molecules are used to split the glucose molecule, glycolysis nets two ATP molecules.

Krebs cycle

The Krebs cycle, also known as the citric acid cycle, is a series of enzyme-controlled chemical reactions that occur in the cell's mitochondria. The Krebs cycle breaks down the pyruvic acid from glycolysis and releases carbon dioxide and ATP. It also releases electrons, which are collected by NAD^+ and other molecules. These electrons are delivered to the electron-transport system.

Electron-transport system

The electron-transport system is a series of enzyme-controlled chemical reactions that occurs in the cell's mitochondria. Through a series of reactions in which oxygen atoms are reduced by accepting the electrons from the Krebs cycle, a large amount of ATP is produced. The oxygen ions join with hydrogen ions to produce water. Most of the ATP produced during cellular respiration occurs in the electron-transport system.

Chemosynthesis

Chemosynthesis is the food-making process of chemoautotrophs in extreme environments such as deep-sea-vents. In general, chemosynthesis involves the oxidation of inorganic substances.

Copyright © Mometrix Media. You have been licensed one copy of this document for personal use only. Any other reproduction or redistribution is strictly prohibited. All rights reserved.

Chemosynthesis is unlike photosynthesis in that chemosynthesis does not require light. Sulfur bacteria live near or in deep-sea vents. Some actually live in other organisms such as huge tube worms near the vents. Hydrogen sulfide is released from deep-sea vents. Instead of sunlight, chemosynthesis uses the energy stored in the chemical bonds of chemicals such as hydrogen sulfide. Carbon is obtained from molecules such as carbon dioxide. During chemosynthesis, the electrons that are removed from the inorganic molecules are combined with carbon possibly from the dissolved carbon dioxide in the seawater or from methane from deep-sea vents to form organic molecules in the form of carbohydrates. Some bacteria use metal ions such as iron and magnesium to obtain the needed electrons. Methanobacteria such as those found in human intestines combine carbon dioxide and hydrogen gas and release methane as a waste product. Nitrogen bacteria such as nitrogen-fixing bacteria in the nodules of legumes convert atmospheric nitrogen into nitrates.

Copyright © Mometrix Media. You have been licensed one copy of this document for personal use only. Any other reproduction or redistribution is strictly prohibited. All rights reserved.

Genetics and Evolution

Law of segregation

The law of segregation states that the alleles for a trait separate when gametes are formed, which means that only one of the pair of alleles for a given trait is passed to the gamete. This can be shown in monohybrid crosses. A monohybrid cross is a genetic cross for a single trait that has two alleles. A monohybrid cross can be used to show which allele is dominant for a single trait. The first monohybrid cross typically occurs between two homozygous parents. Each parent is homozygous for a separate allele for a particular trait. For example, in pea plants, green pods (G) are dominant over yellow pods (g). In a genetic cross of two pea plants that are homozygous for pod color, the F_1 generation will be 100% heterozygous green pods.

	g	g
G	Gg	Gg
G	Gg	Gg

Review Video: Punnett Square
Visit mometrix.com/academy and enter code: 853855

Monohybrid cross for a cross between two Gg parents

If the plants with the heterozygous green pods are crossed, the F_2 generation should be 50% heterozygous green, 25% homozygous green, and 25% homozygous yellow.

	G	g
G	GG	Gg
g	Gg	gg

Law of independent assortment

Mendel's law of independent assortment states that alleles of one characteristic separate independently of the alleles of another characteristic. This means that traits are transmitted independently of each other. This can be shown in dihybrid crosses.

Dihybrid cross for the F2 generation of a cross between GGYY and ggyy parents

A dihybrid cross is a genetic cross for two traits that each have two alleles. For example, in pea plants, green pods (G) are dominant over yellow pods (g), and yellow seeds (Y) are dominant over green seeds (y). In a genetic cross of two pea plants that are homozygous for pod color and seed color, the F_1 generation will be 100% heterozygous green pods and yellow seeds (GgYy). If these F_1 plants are crossed, the resulting F_2 generation is shown below. There are nine genotypes for green-pod, yellow-seed plants: one GGYY, two GGYy, two GgYY, and four GgYy. There are three genotypes for green-pod, green-seed plants: one GGyy and two Ggyy. There are three genotypes for yellow-

- 46 -

Copyright © Mometrix Media. You have been licensed one copy of this document for personal use only. Any other reproduction or redistribution is strictly prohibited. All rights reserved.

pod, yellow-seed plants: one ggYY and two ggYy. There is only one genotype for yellow-pod, green-seed plants: ggyy. This cross has a 9:3:3:1 ratio.

	GY	Gy	gY	gy
GY	GGYY	GGYy	GgYY	GgYy
Gy	GGYy	GGyy	GgYy	Ggyy
gY	GgYY	GgYY	ggYY	ggYy
gy	GgYy	Ggyy	ggYy	ggyy

Pedigree

Pedigree analysis is a type of genetic analysis in which an inherited trait is studied and traced through several generations of a family to determine how that trait is inherited. A pedigree is a chart arranged as a type of family tree using symbols for people and lines to represent the relationships between those people. Squares usually represent males, and circles represent females. Horizontal lines represent a male and female mating, and the vertical lines beneath them represent their children. Usually, family members who possess the trait are fully shaded and those that are carriers only of the trait are half-shaded. Genotypes and phenotypes are determined for each individual if possible. The pedigree below shows the family tree of a family in which the first male who was red-green color blind mated with the first female who was unaffected. They had five children. The three sons were unaffected, and the two daughters were carriers.

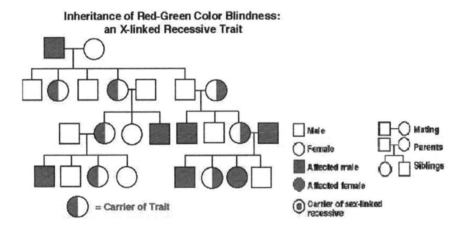

Non-Mendelian inheritance concepts

Linkage

Linkage is an exception to Mendel's law of independent assortment. Linkage can occur when two genes are located on the same chromosome. Each chromosome has several genes, and those genes tend to be inherited together. Genes that are located on the same chromosome and tend to be inherited together are called linkage groups. Because the genes are on the same chromosome, they do not separate during meiosis. During meiosis, the genes in a linkage group always go into the same gamete together. Due to linkage, genes with different characteristics are inherited together more frequently than is predicted using the laws of probability. An example of a linkage group is found on chromosome number 4. This linkage group includes genes for Parkinson's disease, narcolepsy, and Huntington's disease.

- 47 -

Copyright © Mometrix Media. You have been licensed one copy of this document for personal use only. Any other reproduction or redistribution is strictly prohibited. All rights reserved.

Sex-linked inheritance

Sex-linked inheritance is an exception to Mendel's law of independent assortment. In human genetics, females have two X chromosomes, and males have one X and one Y chromosome. Sex-linked traits are carried on the X chromosome. Because females have two X chromosomes, they have two copies of genes found on the X chromosome. Females may possess a recessive allele for various disorders on one X chromosome, but as long as they possess the dominant allele for normal functioning on the other X chromosome, they will not have the disorder. Females who are heterozygous for a trait such as color blindness or hemophilia are only carriers. Because males have only one X chromosome, if they possess the recessive allele for a disorder, it will be expressed. Examples of traits that are a result of sex linkage are color blindness, hemophilia, a form of muscular dystrophy, and some forms of anemia.

Multiple alleles

Multiple alleles result in a type of non-Mendelian inheritance. In Mendelian inheritance, only two alleles for each gene exist. For example, Mendel's pea plants were either tall or short. Mendel's pea plants had either yellow or green pods. Often, there are more than two possibilities for a particular trait. For example, in human genetics, blood type has many variations. Multiple allele inheritance occurs where there are more than two different alleles of a gene for a particular trait. Even though there may be several alleles for a particular trait, each individual can still only possess two of those possible alleles. For example, the three human blood alleles are I^A (blood contains type A antigens), I^B (blood contains type B antigens), and i (blood contains neither type A nor type B antigens).

Blood types and their possible genotypes are shown below.

Blood Type (Phenotype)	Genotype
A	I^AI^A, I^AI^O
B	I^BI^B, I^BI^O
AB	I^AI^B
O	ii

Incomplete dominance

Incomplete dominance is an exception to Mendel's law of dominance. In these situations, there is no dominant or recessive allele. Instead, both alleles of a heterozygote are expressed, and when they are, they blend or mix. For example, there are two alleles for petal color for snapdragons: red (C^R) and white (C^W). Crossing a red snapdragon with a white snapdragon yields an F_1 generation that is 100% heterozygous pink. Crossing two pink snapdragons yields an F_2 generation that is 50% heterozygous pink (C^RC^W), 25% homozygous white (C^WC^W), and 25% homozygous red (C^RC^R).

Laws of dominance and codominance

The law of dominance states that a dominant trait is always expressed. Codominance is an exception to the law of dominance. In codominance, a heterozygote simultaneously expresses both genes for a trait without blending. For example, in certain horses, the hair colors red (D^R) and white (D^W) are codominant. Horses with the genotype D^RD^W have coats composed of red hairs and white hairs, which when mixed together causes their coats to have a golden color.

Copyright © Mometrix Media. You have been licensed one copy of this document for personal use only. Any other reproduction or redistribution is strictly prohibited. All rights reserved.

Polygenic inheritance

Polygenic inheritance occurs when a trait is determined by the interaction of many different genes. In Mendelian genetics, traits are determined by just one pair of genes with two alleles. For example, Mendel's pea plants had either red or white flowers, and his plants were either tall or short. An example of polygenic genetic inheritance in human genetics is skin color and height. Each is controlled by at least four pairs of genes. Skin color has many variations between very light and very dark. Height has many variations between very short and very tall. Eye color and intelligence are also polygenic.

Epistasis

Epistasis occurs when a gene at one locus inhibits the expression of a gene at another locus. For example, in mice, black hair (B) is dominant over brown hair (b). But a different gene at a different locus determines whether or not pigment is deposited (C for deposited and c for not deposited) on the mouse hair. A black mouse with genotypes BB or Bb will only have that color deposited if the pigment genotype is CC or Cc. A black mouse with genotype BBcc will be white. A brown mouse can have genotypes bbCC or bbCc, but a mouse with genotype bbcc will also be white.

Pleiotropy

In Mendelian inheritance, each gene can influence only one trait. Most genes can affect many traits or have multiple phenotypes. Pleiotropy is the situation in which one gene influences several seemingly unrelated traits. A gene that affects multiple traits is pleiotropic. Pleiotropy can be due to normal or mutated genes. Genes code for proteins. Because proteins are often used in more than one tissue or more than one area of the body, a missing protein can cause many complications. For example, the hormone insulin is a protein. If the insulin receptors are faulty, then the cells cannot recognize and use the insulin. Other examples of pleiotropy include inherited diseases such as cystic fibrosis, sickle-cell anemia, phenylketonuria (PKU), and albinism.

Mitochondrial inheritance

Mitochondria are cellular organelles that produce energy for the cell. Mitochondria contain their own DNA consisting of 37 genes arranged in a circular structure. Mitochondrial DNA is transmitted maternally, which means that these mitochondrial genes are only inherited from the mother. The offspring's mitochondria only come from the oocyte (egg cell), not from the sperm. Sperm cells only contain mitochondria in their tails, which does not enter the egg during fertilization. Mitochondrial inheritance is not consistent with Mendelian inheritance in which the zygote derives half of the genetic material from the mother and half from the father. Most of these genes code for proteins related to muscular disorders.

Genetic variation

Mutations

Mutations are one of the main sources of genetic variation. Mutations are changes in DNA. The changes can be gene mutations such as the point mutations of substitution, addition, or deletion, or the changes can be on the chromosomal level such as the chromosomal aberrations of translocations, deletions, inversions, and duplications. Mutations are random and can benefit, harm, or have no effect on the individual. Somatic mutations do not affect inheritance and therefore do not affect genetic variation with regard to evolution. Germline mutations that occur in gametes (eggs and sperm) can be passed to offspring and therefore are very important to genetic variation and evolution. Mutations introduce new genetic information into the genome.

- 49 -

Copyright © Mometrix Media. You have been licensed one copy of this document for personal use only. Any other reproduction or redistribution is strictly prohibited. All rights reserved.

Crossing over

Crossing over is a major source of genetic variation. Crossing over is the exchange of equivalent segments of DNA between homologous chromosomes. Crossing over occurs during meiosis in prophase I. During synapsis, a tetrad is formed when homologous chromosomes pair up. Also during synapsis, the chromatids are extremely close together and sometimes the chromatids swap genes. Because genes have more than one allele, this allows for an exchange of genetic information. Crossing over is that exchange of genes. Crossing over can occur several times along the length of the chromosomes. Although crossing over does not introduce new information, it does introduce new combinations of the information that is available. Without crossing over during meiosis, only two genetically different gametes can be formed. With just one instance of crossing over, four genetically different gametes can be formed. With crossing over, each gamete contains genes from both the father and the mother. Crossing over leads to variation in traits among gametes, which leads to variation in traits among offspring.

Independent assortment during sexual reproduction

Independent assortment during sexual reproduction is a source of genetic variation. Mutations originally brought about changes in DNA leading to alleles or different forms of the same gene. During sexual reproduction, these alleles are "shuffled" or "independently sorted," producing individuals with unique combinations of traits. Gametes are produced during meiosis, which consists of two cell divisions: meiosis I and meiosis II. Meiosis I is a reduction division in which the diploid parent cell divides into two haploid daughter cells. During the metaphase of meiosis I, the homologous pairs (one from the mother and one from the father) align on the equatorial plane. The orientation of the homologous pairs is random, and each placement is independent of another's placement. The number of possible arrangements increases exponentially as the number of chromosomes increases. The independent assortment of chromosomes during metaphase in meiosis I provides a variety of gametes with tremendous differences in their combinations of chromosomes.

> **Review Video: Genes**
> Visit mometrix.com/academy and enter code: 363997
>
> **Review Video: Gene Mutation**
> Visit mometrix.com/academy and enter code: 955485

Chromosomal aberrations

Chromosomal aberrations are changes in DNA sequences on the chromosomal level. These mutations typically involve many genes and often result in miscarriages. Chromosomal aberrations include translocations, deletions, inversions, and duplications. Translocations occur when a piece of DNA breaks off of one chromosome and is joined to another chromosome. Deletions occur when a piece of DNA breaks off on a chromosome and is lost without reattaching. Inversions occur when a piece of DNA breaks off of one chromosome and becomes reattached to that same chromosome but with an inverted or flipped orientation. Duplications occur when a piece of DNA is replicated and attached to the original piece of DNA in sequence.

Chromosomal changes that lead to Down syndrome

Down syndrome is a type of aneuploidy (abnormal number of chromosomes) in which an individual has three copies of chromosome 21, as shown in the karyotype below. When a gamete with an extra 21st chromosome unites with a normal gamete, the result is a group of three chromosomes instead

Copyright © Mometrix Media. You have been licensed one copy of this document for personal use only. Any other reproduction or redistribution is strictly prohibited. All rights reserved.

of a diploid set. A trisomy can occur as a result of nondisjunction, which occurs when a pair of chromosomes fails to separate during meiosis in the formation of an egg or sperm cell.

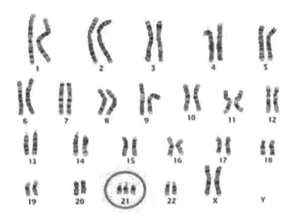

Genetics of sickle-cell anemia

Sickle cell anemia is a genetic disorder that is the result of a gene mutation. Specifically, sickle cell anemia is the result of the point mutation in which adenine is substituted for thymine. This results in a defective form of hemoglobin. Sickle-cell anemia occurs when a person is homozygous for the defective gene. Sickle-cell trait occurs when a person is heterozygous for the defective gene, and this person is a carrier but usually suffers no ill effects. Sickle cell anemia is an example of pleiotropy, in which a change in one gene affects multiple aspects of a person's health. These health problems are due to the abnormally sickle-shaped red blood cells that block the flow of blood, damaging tissues and organs. The sickle-shaped cells tend to rupture, leading to anemia.

Sources of genetic exchange

Genetic exchange, or the transfer of DNA from one organism to another, is a source of genetic variation. Three general types of genetic exchange are transduction, transformation, and conjugation. Transduction occurs when genetic material is transferred from one bacterium to another by a bacteriophage. A bacteriophage is a virus that infects a bacterium. As the new bacteriophages are replicated, some of the host bacteria DNA can be added to the virus particles. Transformation occurs when a cell obtains new genetic information from its environment or surroundings. Many bacteria take up DNA fragments such as plasmids from their surroundings to obtain new genes. Conjugation occurs when bacteria or single-celled organisms are in direct contact with each other. Genes can be transferred from one into the other while the two cells are joined.

Genetic drift

Genetic drift is a microevolutionary process that causes random changes in allele frequencies that are not the result of natural selection. Genetic drift can result in a loss of genetic diversity. Genetic drift greatly impacts small populations. Two special forms of genetic drift are the genetic bottleneck and the founder effect. A genetic bottleneck occurs when there is a drastic reduction in population due to some change such as overhunting, disease, or habitat loss. When a population is greatly reduced in size, many alleles can be lost. Even if the population size greatly increases again, the lost alleles represent lost genetic diversity. The founder effect occurs when one individual or a few individuals populate a new area such as an island. This new population is limited to the alleles of the founder(s) unless mutations occur or new individuals immigrate to the region.

- 51 -

Copyright © Mometrix Media. You have been licensed one copy of this document for personal use only. Any other reproduction or redistribution is strictly prohibited. All rights reserved.

Gene flow

Gene flow is a microevolutionary process in which alleles enter a population by immigration and leave a population by emigration. Gene flow helps counter genetic drift. When individuals from one genetically distinct population immigrate to a different genetically distinct population, alleles and their genetic information are added to the new population. The added alleles will change the gene frequencies within the population. This increases genetic diversity. If individuals with rare alleles emigrate from a population, the genetic diversity is decreased. Gene flow reduces the genetic differences between populations.

HW equilibrium

Hardy–Weinberg (HW) equilibrium is a theoretical concept that uses a mathematical relationship to study gene frequencies. According to HW, if specific conditions are met, the proportions of genotypes in a population can be described by the equation: $p^2 + 2pq + q^2 = 1$, in which p is the frequency of the dominant allele and q is the frequency of the recessive allele. Also, p^2 is the frequency of the homozygous dominant genotype, $2pq$ is the frequency of the heterozygous genotype, and q^2 is the frequency of the homozygous recessive genotype. In addition, the sum of p and q must be equal to one. If the frequencies on the left side of the equation have a sum of one, then the population is in equilibrium, and evolution is not taking place. If the frequencies on the left side of the equation do not have a sum of one, then evolution is taking place. Therefore, the HW equation is only true for populations that are in equilibrium. The HW equilibrium requires the following five conditions to be met: 1) The population must be very large; 2) Mating is random; 3) There are no mutations; 4) No immigration or emigration can occur; and 5) All individuals of the population have an equal chance to survive and reproduce. According to this concept, if all five conditions are met, the gene frequencies will remain constant. In reality, these five conditions are rarely met except in a laboratory situation.

Calculation of allele frequency

> Explain how to calculate allele frequencies of a simple genetic locus at which there are two alleles (A and a) in a population of 1,000 individuals given that the population consists of 120 individuals homozygous for the dominant allele (AA), 480 heterozygous individuals (Aa), and 400 individuals homozygous for the recessive allele (aa).

To calculate the frequency of an allele, divide the total number of those alleles in the population by the total number of alleles in the population for that locus as shown in the following equation:

$$\text{allele frequency} = \frac{\text{total \# of allelles in population}}{\text{total \# of alleles in the population for that locus}}.$$

First, find the total number of each type of allele. The 120 AA individuals produce 240 A alleles. The 480 heterozygous individuals produce 480 A alleles and 480 a alleles. The 400 aa individuals produce 800 a alleles. Therefore, there is a total of 720 A alleles and 1280 a alleles. Adding the 720 and 1,280 yields a total of 2,000 alleles in the population for that locus. The allele frequency for $A = \frac{720}{2,000}$ or 0.36. The allele frequency for $a = \frac{1,280}{2,000}$ or 0.64.

Nucleotide structure

A nucleotide, whether DNA or RNA, contains three components: a phosphate group, a ringed, five-carbon sugar (deoxyribose in DNA, ribose in RNA), and a nitrogen-containing base. The phosphate

Copyright © Mometrix Media. You have been licensed one copy of this document for personal use only. Any other reproduction or redistribution is strictly prohibited. All rights reserved.

group binds to one side of the ringed, five-carbon sugar. The nitrogen-containing base binds to the opposite side of the ringed, five-carbon sugar. A nucleotide strand is formed by covalently linking the phosphate groups of the nucleotides into a linear sequence.

DNA Nucleotide Structure

DNA and RNA

Structural similarities

Structural similarities between DNA and RNA:

- DNA and RNA are both nucleic acids composed of nucleotides made up of a sugar, a base, and a phosphate molecule.
- DNA and RNA have three of their four bases in common: guanine, cytosine, and adenine.

Structural differences, location, and function

Structural differences between DNA and RNA:

- DNA contains the base thymine, but RNA replaces thymine with uracil.
- DNA contains the sugar deoxyribose, but RNA contains the sugar ribose.
- DNA is double stranded, but RNA is single stranded.

Location – DNA is located in the nucleus and mitochondria. RNA is found in the nucleus, ribosomes, and cytoplasm.

Function – DNA contains the genetic blueprint and instructions for the cell. RNA carries out those instructions.

Types and functions of RNA

Types of RNA include ribosomal RNA (rRNA), transfer RNA (tRNA), and messenger RNA (mRNA).

- rRNA: forms the RNA component of the ribosome. It is evolutionarily conserved, which means it can be used to study relationships in organisms.
- mRNA: used by the ribosome to generate proteins (translation). The mRNA contains three-nucleotide "codons" that code for specific amino acids in a protein sequence.
- tRNA: functions in translation by carrying an amino acid to the corresponding codon on the mRNA strand.

- 53 -

Copyright © Mometrix Media. You have been licensed one copy of this document for personal use only. Any other reproduction or redistribution is strictly prohibited. All rights reserved.

Review Video: DNA
Visit mometrix.com/academy and enter code: 639552

Review Video: DNA Mutations
Visit mometrix.com/academy and enter code: 822061

Review Video: DNA Replication
Visit mometrix.com/academy and enter code: 128118

Complementary base pairing

According to Chargaff's rule, DNA always has a 1:1 ratio of purine to pyrimidine. The amount of adenine always equals the amount of thymine, and the amount of guanine always equals the amount of cytosine. DNA contains the bases guanine, cytosine, thymine, and adenine. RNA also contains guanine, cytosine, and adenine, but thymine is replaced with uracil. In DNA, adenine always pairs with thymine, and guanine always pairs with cytosine. In RNA, adenine always pairs with uracil, and guanine always pairs with cytosine. The pairs are bonded together with hydrogen bonds.

Double helix structure of DNA

Double-stranded DNA consists of two complimentary strands that adopt the shape of a double helix, which resembles a twisted ladder. The "sides" of the ladder are the phosphate backbones of the complimentary strands. The "rungs" of the ladder are the sugar-base components, which are held together (base paired) by hydrogen bonds between the nitrogenous bases in opposite strands. In DNA, adenine (A) base pairs with thymine (T) and guanine (G) base pairs with cytosine (C).

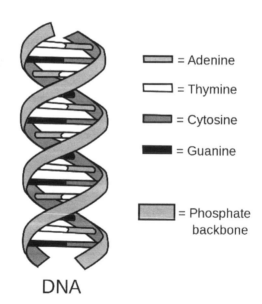

DNA

Organization of prokaryotic DNA

Prokaryotes lack distinct a nucleus with DNA. Prokaryotic DNA is organized primarily into a central loop contained in the cytoplasm. Prokaryotes may also contain smaller loops of DNA known as plasmids that contain other genes. Most prokaryotes lack histones. Archae are an example of prokaryotes that do contain histones.

Copyright © Mometrix Media. You have been licensed one copy of this document for personal use only. Any other reproduction or redistribution is strictly prohibited. All rights reserved.

Organization of eukaryotic DNA

Eukaryotes have a nucleus with multiple chromosomes, each containing a tightly-compacted, double-helix DNA molecule. The structural sub-components of chromosomes include histones, nucleosomes, and chromatin.

- Histones are positively-charged, DNA-binding proteins.
- A nucleosome is composed of eight histone proteins around which approximately 146 base pairs of DNA are wrapped. The nucleosome is often called a "beads on a string" structure.
- Chromatin is made up of compacted nucleosomes.
- Chromosomes are made up of compacted chromatin.

RNA is also thought to play a role in chromatin structure.

Telomeres

Eukaryotic chromosomes have telomeres located at their tips. Telomeres are repetitive sequences of DNA that maintain the ends of the linear chromosomes and keep those ends from deteriorating.

DNA replication

DNA replication begins when the double strands of the parent DNA molecule are unwound and unzipped. The enzyme helicase separates the two strands by breaking the hydrogen bonds between the base pairs that make up the rungs of the twisted ladder. These two single strands of DNA are called the replication fork. Each separate DNA strand provides a template for the complementary DNA bases, G with C and A with T. The opposite ends of DNA are called the 5' and 3' ends. After the DNA is separated, the enzyme RNA primase lays down an RNA primer that the enzyme DNA polymerase binds to initiate replication. DNA polymerase replicates DNA from the 3' end towards the 5' end. Of the two strands open during replication, the strand with the 3' end will be replicated as a single, continuous leading strand. The strand with the 5' end will be replicated into shorter, unlinked segments known as Okizaki fragments. The enzyme RNAse removes the RNA primers used to initiate replication of the two strands. A separate DNA polymerase fills in gaps after the RNA primer is removed. The Okizaki fragments are joined by the enzyme DNA ligase.

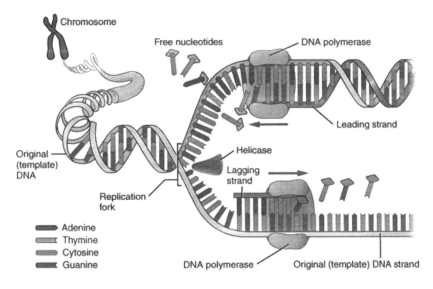

Copyright © Mometrix Media. You have been licensed one copy of this document for personal use only. Any other reproduction or redistribution is strictly prohibited. All rights reserved.

Transcription

Transcription is the process by which a segment of DNA is copied onto a working blueprint called RNA. Each gene has a special region called a promoter that guides the beginning of the transcription process. RNA polymerase unwinds the DNA at the promoter region and makes an RNA copy of the DNA gene by adding the complementary nucleotides, G with C , C with G, T with A, and A with U. This forms a single strand of messenger RNA or mRNA.

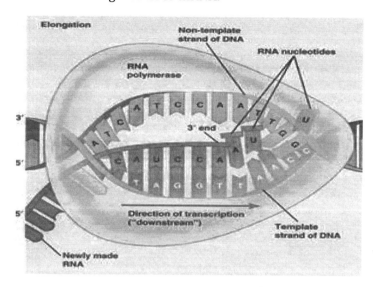

Processing mRNA

In addition to being transcribed, the mRNA must also be processed. First, a 5' cap (modified guanine nucleotide) is added, which helps promote ribosome recognition and preventing mRNA degradation. Second, a string of adenosine ribonucleotides are added to the 3' end of the mRNA, forming a structure known as a poly(A) tail. The poly(A) tail helps prevent mRNA degradation. The mRNA transcript may contain regions that do not code for protein, called introns. The regions that do code for protein are called exons. If introns are present, they will be removed in a process called splicing by a structure known as the spliceosome. After addition of the 5' cap, addition of the poly(A) tail, and splicing, the mRNA is ready for translation.

Translation

Ribosomes synthesize proteins from mRNA in a process called translation. The ribosome has three tRNA binding sites—A, P, and E. Translation initiates when the "A site" becomes occupied by the tRNA molecule corresponding to the mRNA start codon. The ribosome then moves the first tRNA from the "A site" to the "P site." The "A site" is then occupied by the tRNA molecule corresponding to the second mRNA codon. The ribosome then transfers the amino acid on the "P site" tRNA to the amino acid on the "A site" tRNA. The first tRNA, which now has no amino acid, is moved from the "P site" the "E site." The second tRNA, complexed to a chain of two amino acids, is moved from the "A site" to the "P site." The "A site" is then occupied by the tRNA corresponding to the third mRNA codon. The "P site" amino acid chain is transferred to the amino acid bound to the "A site" tRNA. The first tRNA then exits from the "E site" and the second and third tRNA molecules shift, opening the "A site" for the next tRNA. The growing amino acid chain continues to be transferred from the "P site" to the "A site" until translation is complete.

- 56 -

Copyright © Mometrix Media. You have been licensed one copy of this document for personal use only. Any other reproduction or redistribution is strictly prohibited. All rights reserved.

Regulation of gene expression

Role of promoters

Promoters are DNA sequences located upstream of the gene needed for transcription. Promoters signal the beginning of transcription. Special proteins called transcription factors, which bind to promoters, subsequently provide binding sites for the RNA polymerase, which is the enzyme that transcribes the RNA. Promoters in the Archaea and Eukaryota domains often contain a nucleotide sequence TATA, which is called a TATA box. The TATA box is usually 25 nucleotides upstream of the transcription start site, and it is the location at which the DNA is unwound.

Role of enhancers

Enhancers are DNA sequences that regulate gene expression by providing a binding site for proteins that regulate RNA polymerase in transcribing proteins. Enhancers can greatly increase the expression of genes in their range. They can be hundreds or thousands of base pairs upstream or downstream from the genes they control. Some enhancers are located within the gene they control. Enhancers are functional over large distances. Most genes are controlled by two or three enhancers, but some may be controlled by more. Enhancers provide binding sites for regulatory proteins that either promote or inhibit RNA polymerase activity. Enhancers are more common in eukaryotes than prokaryotes.

Role of transcription factors

Transcription factors are DNA-binding proteins that help regulate gene expression in eukaryotes and prokaryotes. In eukaryotes that have promoter or enhancer regions, transcription factors bind near these regions and increase the ability of the RNA polymerase to start transcription. In eukaryotes, because genes are typically turned "off," transcription factors typically work to turn genes "on." The opposite is often true in bacteria, and transcription factors often work to turn genes off.

Role of operons

Operons are segments of DNA or groups of genes that are controlled by one promoter. Operons consist of an operator, a promoter, and structural gene(s). The operator provides a binding side for a repressor that inhibits the binding of RNA polymerase. The promoter provides the binding site for the RNA polymerase. The structural genes provide the sequence that codes for a protein. Operons are transcribed as single units and code for a single mRNA molecule, which produces proteins with related functions. Operons have been found in prokaryotes, eukaryotes, and viruses. For example, the lac (lactose) operon in certain bacteria controls the production of the enzymes needed to digest lactose. If lactose is already available in the cell, the lactose binds to the repressor protein to prevent the repressor protein from binding to the operator. The gene is transcribed, and the enzymes necessary for the digestion of the lactose are produced. If there is no lactose that needs to be digested, the repressor protein binds to the operator. The gene is not transcribed, and the enzyme is not produced. This allows the cell to only code for proteins as needed by the cell.

Role of epigenetics

Epigenetics studies factors or mechanisms that determine if genes are active (switched on) or dormant (switched off). These mechanisms can alter gene function or gene expression without altering the sequences of the DNA itself. An example is the addition of a methyl group (methylation) to the histones. Acetylation, the addition of an acetyl group, and phosphorylation, the addition of a phosphoryl group, are also modifications to the proteins associated with DNA that can switch genes on or off or affect their activity level.

Copyright © Mometrix Media. You have been licensed one copy of this document for personal use only. Any other reproduction or redistribution is strictly prohibited. All rights reserved.

Differential gene expression

Differential gene expression is the expression of different sets of gene by cells with identical DNA molecules. The unused genes in a differentiated cell remain in the cell but are not expressed. Actually, only a few genes are expressed in each cell. For example, during mammalian embryonic development, the undifferentiated zygote undergoes cell division through mitosis. As the number of cells increases, selected cells undergo differentiation to become specialized components in the developing tissues of the embryo.

Stem cells

Stem cells are undifferentiated cells that can divide without limit and that can differentiate to produce the specialized cells that each organism needs. Embryonic stem cells are harvested from the embryo at the blastocyst stage or from the developing gonads of the embryo. Stem cells can be pluripotent or multipotent depending on their source. Early embryonic stem cells are pluripotent. This means they have not undergone any differentiation and have the ability to become any special type of cell. After embryonic stem cells begin to differentiate, they may be limited to specializing into a specific tissue type. These stem cells are considered to be multipotent because they can only develop into a few different types of cells. Adult stem cells, also called somatic stem cells, are harvested from organs and tissues and can differentiate into those types of cells in that particular organ or tissue. Umbilical cord blood stem cells can be harvested from the umbilical cord of a newborn baby. Adult stem cells and umbilical cord blood stem cells are multipotent. Induced pluripotent cells (iPS) are somatic cells that have been manipulated to act like pluripotent cells. Experiments have shown that iPS may be useful in treating diseases.

Mutations

Missense mutatinos, silent mutations, and nonsense mutations

Mutations are changes in DNA sequences. Point mutations are changes in a single nucleotide in a DNA sequence. Three types of point mutations are missense, silent, and nonsense.

- Missense mutations result in a codon for a different amino acid. An example is mutating TGT (Cysteine codon) to TGG (Tryptophan codon).
- Silent mutations result in a codon for the same amino acid as the original sequence. An example is mutating TGT (Cysteine codon) to TGC (a different Cysteine codon).
- Nonsense mutations insert a premature stop codon, typically resulting in a non-functional protein. An example is mutating TGT (Cysteine codon) to TGA (STOP codon).

Frameshift mutations and inversion mutations

Deletions and insertions can result in the addition of amino acids, the removal of amino acids, or cause a frameshift mutation. A frameshift mutation changes the reading frame of the mRNA (a new group of codons will be read), resulting in the formation of a new protein product. Mutations can also occur on the chromosomal level. For example, an inversion is when a piece of the chromosome inverts or flips its orientation.

Germline mutations and somatic mutations

Mutations can occur in somatic (body) cells and germ cells (egg and sperm). Somatic mutations develop after conception and occur in an organism's body cells such as bone cells, liver cells, or brain cells. Somatic mutations cannot be passed on from parent to offspring. The mutation is limited to the specific descendent of the cell in which the mutation occurred. The mutation is not in the other body cells unless they are descendants of the originally mutated cell. Somatic mutations

- 58 -

Copyright © Mometrix Media. You have been licensed one copy of this document for personal use only. Any other reproduction or redistribution is strictly prohibited. All rights reserved.

may cause cancer or diseases. Some somatic mutations are silent. Germline mutations are present at conception and occur in an organism's germ cells, which are only egg and sperms cells. Germline mutations may be passed on from parent to offspring. Germline mutations will be present in every cell of an offspring that inherits a germline mutation. Germline mutations may cause diseases. Some germline mutations are silent.

Mutagens

Mutagens are physical and chemical agents that cause changes or errors in DNA replication. Mutagens are external factors to an organism. Examples include ionizing radiation such as ultraviolet radiation, x-rays, and gamma radiation. Viruses and microorganisms that integrate their DNA into host chromosomes are also mutagens. Mutagens include environmental poisons such as asbestos, coal tars, tobacco, and benzene. Alcohol and diets high in fat have been shown to be mutagenic. Not all mutations are caused by mutagens. Spontaneous mutations can occur in DNA due to molecular decay.

PCR

The polymerase chain reaction (PCR) is a laboratory technique used to rapidly copy selected segments of DNA. PCR can be performed on the DNA from a single cell. PCR is a hot-and-cold cycled reaction that uses a special heat-tolerant polymerase. The DNA sample is combined with this special DNA polymerase, primers, and free nucleotides. Primers are synthetic strands of DNA containing just a few bases. The first step is a high-temperature denaturation step (90–95°C) that causes the DNA strands to unwind. The second step is a low-temperature annealing step (~60°C) in which the primers anneal to the single-stranded DNA. The final step is an activation step that matches the activation temperature for the heat-resistant DNA polymerase (~70°C, depending on the enzyme). This final step results in the formation of newly-synthesized, double-stranded DNA. These steps will be repeated on the same sample for multiple cycles, typically ~30. The number of DNA copies generated is 2^N, where N is the number of cycles.

DNA sequencing

DNA sequencing is a laboratory technique used to determine the order or linear sequence of nucleotides of DNA fragments. A polymerase chain reaction (PCR) is used to isolate the needed DNA segment or DNA template. During PCR, some of each of the nucleotides containing the four bases, G, C, A, and T, is chemically altered and fluorescently tagged with different colors of dye. Also, the chemically altered nucleotides have the dideoxyribose sugar, which contains one less oxygen atom than the usual deoxyribose. When synthesis begins, the polymerase randomly adds either a regular nucleotide or an altered nucleotide. If the polymerase adds an altered nucleotide, synthesis stops. This way, each DNA fragment of the same length is tagged with the same color. Then, electrophoresis is used to separate DNA fragments according to length. The DNA sequence can be read by reading the tags of the shortest fragments to the tags of the longest fragments.

Human Genome Project

In 1990, the Human Genome Project (HGP), which involved scientists from 16 laboratories located in at least 6 different countries, was launched to map the human genome. The project was completed in 2003. The human genome consists of approximately 3.12 billion paired nucleotides. The genomes of several plants, animal, fungi, protists, bacteria, viruses, and even cell organelles have also been studied and mapped. Interesting comparisons can be made between these genomes. For example, the number of genes in an organism's genome does not indicate the complexity of that

Copyright © Mometrix Media. You have been licensed one copy of this document for personal use only. Any other reproduction or redistribution is strictly prohibited. All rights reserved.

organism. Humans have approximately 21,000 genes, but the simpler roundworms have approximately 26,000 genes.

Gene therapy

Gene therapy is an experimental but promising technique that introduces new genes into an organism to correct a specific disease caused by a defective gene. In gene therapy, the defective gene is replaced by a properly functioning gene. Gene therapy is most promising for diseases that are caused by a single defective gene. For example, gene therapy was first successfully used to treat severe combined immunodeficiency (SCID). One type of SCID is caused by a single defective gene on the X chromosome. Doctors removed some bone marrow from the test subjects, injected a retrovirus that was carrying the gene, and then re-implanted the bone marrow. The bone marrow cells then have the correct DNA sequence for the production of proteins for much needed enzymes. Unfortunately, some of the first recipients developed leukemia, and the trials were halted. Later, researchers discovered that the leukemia was related to the location of the insertion of the retroviral vectors.

Cloning

Clones are exact biological copies of genes, cells, or multicellular organisms. There are natural clones and artificial clones. Many clones are produced in nature. Animals that can reproduce asexually by fragmentation or budding produce natural clones. Some plants such as strawberries can reproduce by stolons. Typically, in biology, cloning refers to gene cloning or the cloning of organisms. Gene cloning is the process of splicing genes that are needed to code for a specific protein and introducing them into a new cell with a DNA vector. Gene cloning has been used with bacteria in the production of human insulin and a human growth hormone replacement.

Cloning can also occur with an entire organism. This type of cloning is called a somatic cell nuclear transfer. The first mammal clone was Dolly the sheep. In this procedure, a nucleus of a somatic cell from the sheep to be cloned was transferred or injected into a denucleated egg cell of the surrogate mother sheep. The egg was stimulated to divide by electric shock, and then the embryo was implanted into the uterus of the surrogate mother. Dolly was born identical to the egg nucleus donor, not the surrogate mother. Dolly and other cloned mammals typically have serious health problems. Dolly aged prematurely possibly due to the shortened telomeres from the adult somatic cell nucleus.

Genetic engineering and genetically engineered cells

Genetic engineering is the manipulation of DNA outside of normal reproduction. This modified DNA is called recombinant DNA. Genetic engineering is prevalent in gene cloning, which is used in the production of genetically modified (GM) organisms and the production of GM food. Gene cloning involves cloning a specific gene that is needed for a specific purpose. Genes can be inserted into cells of an entirely different species. Genetically engineered cells are also called transgenic cells. GM organisms such plants or crops contain recombinant DNA. Many types of organisms such as plants, animals, fungi, and bacteria have been genetically modified. GM crops such as corn and soybeans can be engineered to be herbicide resistant to ensure that herbicides kill the weeds but not the crop plants. Crops can also be modified to be pest resistant in order to kill the insects that might damage the crops. Also, several foods can be genetically modified to increase nutritional value.

- 60 -

Copyright © Mometrix Media. You have been licensed one copy of this document for personal use only. Any other reproduction or redistribution is strictly prohibited. All rights reserved.

Mechanisms of evolution

Natural and artificial selection

Natural selection and artificial selection are both mechanisms of evolution. Natural selection is a process of nature. Natural selection is the way in which a population can change over generations. Every population has variations in individual heritable traits. Not all individuals of a population reproduce. The organisms best suited for survival typically reproduce and pass on their genetic traits. Typically, the more advantageous a trait is, the more common that trait becomes in a population. Natural selection brings about evolutionary adaptations and is responsible for biological diversity. Artificial selection is another mechanism of evolution. Artificial selection is a process brought about by humans. Artificial selection is the selective breeding of domesticated animals and plants such as when farmers choose animals or plants with desirable traits to reproduce. Artificial selection has led to the evolution of farm stock and crops. For example, cauliflower, broccoli, and cabbage all evolved due to artificial selection of the wild mustard plant.

Sexual selection

Sexual selection is a special case of natural selection in animal populations. Sexual selection occurs because some animals are more likely to find mates than other animals. The two main contributors to sexual selection are competition of males and mate selection by females. An example of male competition is in the mating practices of the redwing blackbird. Some males have huge territories and numerous mates that they defend. Other males have small territories, and some even have no mates. An example of mate selection by females is the mating practices of peacocks. Male peacocks display large, colorful tail feathers to attract females. Females are more likely to choose males with the larger, more colorful displays.

Coevolution

Coevolution describes a rare phenomenon in which two populations with a close ecological relationship undergo reciprocal adaptations simultaneously and evolve together, affecting each other's evolution. General examples of coevolution include predator and prey, or plant and pollinator, and parasites and their hosts. A specific example of coevolution is the yucca moths and the yucca plants. Yucca plants can only be pollinated by the yucca moths. The yucca moths lay their eggs in the yucca flowers, and their larvae grow inside the ovary.

Adaptive radiation

Adaptive radiation is an evolutionary process in which a species branches out and adapts and fills numerous unoccupied ecological niches. The adaptations occur relatively quickly, driven by natural selection and resulting in new phenotypes and possibly new species eventually. An example of adaptive radiation is the finches that Darwin studied on the Galápagos Islands. Darwin recorded 13 different varieties of finches, which differed in the size and shape of their beaks. Through the process of natural selection, each type of finch adapted to the specific environment and specifically the food sources of the island to which it belonged. On newly formed islands with many unoccupied ecological niches, the adaptive radiation process occurred quickly due to the lack of competing species and predators.

> **Review Video: Organic Evolution**
> Visit mometrix.com/academy and enter code: 108959

Copyright © Mometrix Media. You have been licensed one copy of this document for personal use only. Any other reproduction or redistribution is strictly prohibited. All rights reserved.

Evidence supporting evolution

Molecular evidence

Because all organisms are made up of cells, all organisms are alike on a fundamental level. Cells share similar components, which are made up of molecules. Specifically, all cells contain DNA and RNA. This should indicate that all species descended from a common ancestor. Humans and chimpanzees share approximately 98% of their genes in common, and humans and bacteria share approximately 7% of their genes in common. Humans and zebra fish share approximately 85% of their genes in common. Humans and mustard greens share approximately 15% of their genes in common. Biologists have been able to use DNA sequence comparisons of modern organisms to reconstruct the "root" of the tree of life. The fact that RNA can store information, replicate itself, and code for proteins suggests that RNA could have could have evolved first, followed by DNA.

Homology

Homology is the similarity of structures of different species based on a similar structure in a common evolutionary ancestor. The forelimbs of whales, frogs, horses, lions, humans, bats, and birds all have the same basic pattern of the bones. Specifically, all of these organisms have a humerus, radius, and ulna. Tetrapods all have limbs with five digits at some stage in their development. For example, embryonic birds start with limbs with five digits, but adult bird wings have only three digits. They are all modifications of the same basic evolutionary structure from a common ancestor. Tetrapods resemble the fossils of extinct transitional animal called the *Eusthenopteron*. This would seem to indicate that evolution primarily modifies preexisting structures.

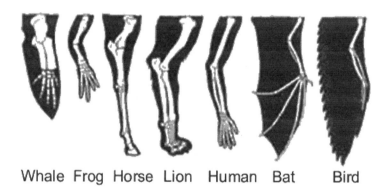

Whale Frog Horse Lion Human Bat Bird

Embryology

The stages of embryonic development reveal homologies between species. These homologies are evidence of a common ancestor. For example, in chicken embryos and mammalian embryos, both include a stage in which slits and arches appear in the embryo's neck region that are strikingly similar to gill slits and gill arches in fish embryos. Adult chickens and adult mammals do not have gills, but this embryonic homology indicates that birds and mammals share a common ancestor with fish. As another example, some species of toothless whales have embryos that initially develop teeth that are later absorbed, which indicates that these whales have an ancestor with teeth in the adult form. Finally, most tetrapods have five-digit limbs, but birds have three-digit limbs in their wings. However, embryonic birds initially have five-digit limbs in their wings, which develop into a three-digit wing. Tetrapods such as reptiles, mammals, and birds all share a common ancestor with five-digit limbs.

Copyright © Mometrix Media. You have been licensed one copy of this document for personal use only. Any other reproduction or redistribution is strictly prohibited. All rights reserved.

Endosymbiosis theory

The endosymbiosis theory is foundational to evolution. Endosymbiosis provides the path for prokaryotes to give rise to eukaryotes. Specifically, endosymbiosis explains the development of the organelles of mitochondria in animals and chloroplasts in plants. This theory states that some eukaryotic organelles such as mitochondria and chloroplasts originated as free living cells. According to this theory, primitive, heterotrophic eukaryotes engulfed smaller, autotrophic bacteria prokaryotes, but the bacteria were not digested. Instead, the eukaryotes and the bacteria formed a symbiotic relationship. Eventually, the bacteria transformed into mitochondrion or chloroplasts.

<u>Supporting evidence</u>

Several facts support the endosymbiosis theory. Mitochondria and chloroplasts contain their own DNA and can both only arise from other preexisting mitochondria and chloroplasts. The genomes of mitochondria and chloroplasts consist of single, circular DNA molecules with no histones. This is similar to bacteria genomes, not eukaryote genomes. Also, the RNA, ribosomes, and protein synthesis of mitochondria and chloroplasts are remarkably similar to those of bacteria, and both use oxygen to produce ATP. These organelles have a double phospholipid layer that is typical of engulfed bacteria. This theory also involves a secondary endosymbiosis in which the original eukaryotic cells that have engulfed the bacteria are then engulfed themselves by another free-living eukaryote.

Convergent evolution

Convergent evolution is the evolutionary process in which two or more unrelated species become increasingly similar in appearance. In convergent evolution, natural selection leads to adaptation in these unrelated species belonging to the same kind of environment. For example, the mammals shown below, although found in different parts of the world, developed similar appearances due to their similar environments.

Divergent evolution

Divergent evolution is the evolutionary process in which organisms of one species become increasingly dissimilar in appearance. As several small adaptations occur due to natural selection, the organisms will finally reach a point at which two new species are formed. Then, these two species will further diverge from each other as they continue to evolve. Adaptive radiation is an

- 63 -

Copyright © Mometrix Media. You have been licensed one copy of this document for personal use only. Any other reproduction or redistribution is strictly prohibited. All rights reserved.

example of divergent evolution. Another example is the divergent evolution of the wooly mammoth and the modern elephant from a common ancestor.

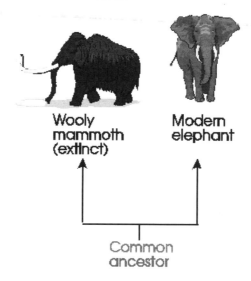

Fossil record

The fossil record provides many types of support for evolution including comparisons from rock layers, transition fossils, and homologies with modern organisms. First, fossils from rock layers from all over the world have been compared, enabling scientists to develop a sequence of life from simple to complex. Based on the fossil record, the geologic timeline chronicles the history of all living things. For example, the fossil record clearly indicates that invertebrates developed before vertebrates and that fish developed before amphibians. Second, numerous transitional fossils have been found. Transitional fossils show an intermediate state between an ancestral form of an organism and the form of its descendants. These fossils show the path of evolutionary change. For example, many transition fossils documenting the evolutionary change from fish to amphibians have been discovered. In 2004, scientists discovered *Tiktaalik roseae*, or the "fishapod," which is a 375-million-year-old fossil that exhibits both fish and amphibian characteristics. For example, scientists have determined that *Pakicetus,* an extinct land mammal, is an early ancestor of modern whales and dolphins based on the specialized structures of the inner ear. Most fossils exhibit homologies with modern organisms. For example, extinct horses are similar to modern horses, indicating a common ancestor.

Cephalization

Two major evolutionary trends are cephalization and multicellularity. Cephalization is the evolutionary trend that can be summarized as "the evolution of the head." In most animals, nerve tissue has been concentrated into a brain at one end of an organism over many generations. Eventually, a head enclosing a brain and housing sensory organs was produced at one end of the organism. Many invertebrates, such as arthropods and annelids and all vertebrates, have undergone cephalization. However, some invertebrates, such as echinoderms and sponges, have not undergone cephalization, and these organisms literally do not have a head.

Multicellularity

Another evolutionary trend is multicellularity. Life has evolved from simple, single-celled organisms to complex, multicellular organisms. Over millions of years, single-celled organisms gave

- 64 -

Copyright © Mometrix Media. You have been licensed one copy of this document for personal use only. Any other reproduction or redistribution is strictly prohibited. All rights reserved.

rise to biofilms, which gave rise to multicellular organisms, which gave rise to all of the major phyla of multicellular organisms present today..

Speciation

Significance of reproductive isolation

Biological species are groups of organisms that can breed and produce viable offspring. New species may originate due to reproductive isolation between members of the same species. Prezygotic barriers occur before fertilization and stop or hinder species from mating. Postzygotic barriers occur after fertilization but prevent the hybrids from living or being fertile. If gene flow between two groups of a species is hindered or stopped completely, more significant genetic differences between the two groups can accumulate. In order for speciation to occur, differences between two incipient or emerging species must occur. For the two incipient species to completely split, one of two things must occur. Either mating between the incipient species cannot occur, or the offspring must be nonviable or sterile. These situations can occur in many ways. For example, a change in the mating location or a change in the mating rituals can keep mating from occurring. Changes dues to natural selection or genetic drift may affect mating or viability of offspring. Various modes of geographic and population isolation may occur, but the key to speciation in each type is still the reduced gene flow.

Modes

Speciation has various modes that bring about the reduced gene flow needed for incipient species to fully separate. Allopatric speciation occurs between two incipient species that become geographically isolated populations. Say, for some geographic reason, two or more groups within a species cannot mate with each other. This could be due to a volcanic eruption, a desert, or a river. Some may still mate, but the gene flow is greatly reduced. Peripatric speciation is a more specific type of allopatric speciation. Peripatric speciation occurs when an extremely small group is geographically isolated at the edge of the rest of the population. This small population size brings about genetic drift relatively quickly. Parapatric speciation occurs within a continuously distributed population. This occurs due to a geographic distance instead of a geographic barrier. Individuals in the population simply choose to mate with close neighbors, leading to a reduced gene flow. Natural selection in the range of those individuals brings about further differentiation among members of the species spread out across the population. Sympatric speciation occurs when a new species develops within a population with no geographic isolation. Sympatric speciation is uncommon but may occur when a species inhabits a new niche.

Models of evolutionary rates

Gradualism

Gradualism is a model of evolutionary rates that states that evolutionary changes occurred slowly or gradually by a divergence of lineages due largely to natural selection. These accumulated changes occurred over millions of years. Many transitional forms occurred between ancestors and modern descendants. Although not all of these transitional forms were preserved in the fossil record, the fossil record clearly supports gradualism. Many transition fossils show adaptations as organisms evolve. The geologic time scale describes this gradual change from simple to complex organisms over millions of years.

Punctuated equilibrium

Punctuated equilibrium is a model of evolutionary rates that states that in some instances, evolutionary changes occurred in relatively short burst that "punctuate" long periods of

Copyright © Mometrix Media. You have been licensed one copy of this document for personal use only. Any other reproduction or redistribution is strictly prohibited. All rights reserved.

equilibrium of little or no change. These "short" periods would still consist of hundreds of thousands of years. Most scientists believe that punctuated equilibrium occurred along with gradualism. The fossil record supports punctuated equilibrium for many organisms. Punctuated equilibrium provides an explanation for the supposed numerous "missing links" in the fossil record. If punctuated equilibrium is validated, then there actually are no missing links.

Explanations for the origin of life on Earth

Panspermia

The word *panspermia* is a Greek work that means "seeds everywhere." Panspermia is one possible explanation for the origin of life on Earth that states that "seeds" of life exist throughout the universe and can be transferred from one location to another. Three types of panspermia based on the seed-dispersal method have been proposed. Lithopanspermia is described as rocks transferring microorganisms between solar systems. Ballistic panspermia is described as rocks transferring microorganisms within a solar system. Directed panspermia is described as intelligent extraterrestrials spreading the seeds to other planets and solar systems. The panspermia hypothesis only proposes the origin of life on Earth. It does not offer an explanation for the origin of life in the universe or explain the origin of the seeds themselves.

Abiotic synthesis of organic compounds

Scientists have performed sophisticated experiments to determine how the first organic compounds appeared on Earth. First, scientists performed controlled experiments that closely resembled the conditions similar to an early Earth. In the classic Miller–Urey experiment (1953), the Earth's early atmosphere was simulated with water, methane, ammonia, and hydrogen that were stimulated by an electric discharge. The Miller–Urey experiment produced complex organic compounds including several amino acids, sugars, and hydrocarbons. Later experiments by other scientists produced nucleic acids. Recently, Jeffrey Bada, a former student of Miller, was able to produce amino acids in a simulation using the Earth's current atmospheric conditions with the addition of iron and carbonate to the simulation. This is significant because in previous studies using Earth's current atmosphere, the amino acids were destroyed by the nitrites produced by the nitrogen.

Atmospheric composition

The early atmosphere of Earth had little or possibly no oxygen. Early rocks had high levels of iron at their surfaces. Without oxygen, the iron just entered into the early oceans as ions. In the same time frame, early photosynthetic algae were beginning to grow abundantly in the early ocean. During photosynthesis, the algae would produce oxygen gas, which oxidized the iron at the rocks' surfaces, forming an iron oxide. This process basically kept the algae in an oxygen-free environment. As the algae population grew much larger, it eventually produced such a large amount of oxygen that it could not be removed by the iron in the rocks. Because the algae at this time were intolerant to oxygen, the algae became extinct. Over time, a new iron-rich layer of sediments formed, and algae populations reformed, and the cycle began again. This cycle repeated itself for millions of years. Iron-rich layers of sediment alternated with iron-poor layers. Gradually, algae and other life forms evolved that were tolerant to oxygen, stabilizing the oxygen concentration in the atmosphere at levels similar to those of today.

Copyright © Mometrix Media. You have been licensed one copy of this document for personal use only. Any other reproduction or redistribution is strictly prohibited. All rights reserved.

Development of self-replication

Several theories for the origin of life involve the self-replication of molecules. In order for life to have originated on Earth, proteins and RNA must have been replicated. Theories that combine the replication of proteins and RNA seem promising. One such theory is called RNA world. RNA world explains how the pathway of DNA to RNA to protein may have originated by proposing the reverse process. In RNA world, RNA is the precursor to DNA. Scientists have shown that RNA can actually function both as a gene and as an enzyme. Also, RNA can be transcribed into DNA. In RNA world, RNA molecules self-replicated and evolved through recombination and mutations. RNA molecules developed the ability to act as enzymes. Eventually, RNA began to synthesize proteins. Finally, DNA molecules were copied from the RNA in a process of reverse transcription.

Causes of extinction of species

Lack of genetic diversity

Genetic diversity provides a mechanism for populations to adapt to changing environments or even human impacts. With a diverse genome, individuals possessing genes making them better suited for the environment are more likely to exist. Without genetic diversity, populations cannot develop adaptations. Populations cannot resist diseases or adapt to changes in the habitat. As the populations of endangered species decrease, genetic diversity decreases even further. Normally, natural selection selects genes that resist diseases or help the organism to adapt to changes in the habitat, but if those genes have drifted out of the population, the population cannot evolve and may become extinct. A small gene pool does not provide much variety for selection. For example, tigers in India are now in danger of extinction. Studies show that more than 90% of the genome has been lost largely due to a period when tigers were heavily killed by British officials and Indian royalty. With fewer than 2,000 tigers in the world and these in small populations, the genetic diversity can continue to decrease, possibly leading to extinction if much effort is not made to preserve the remaining genetic diversity.

Environmental pressures

A changing environment may lead to the extinction of a species. If an animal has a small tolerance range to food sources and habitat needs or if a population is small, it is less likely to adapt to changes in the environment. Climate change and global warming can affect an ecosystem. Some species may not be able to adapt even to seemingly minor temperature changes especially if their populations are small. Animals needing cooler climates may need to move to cooler habitats. Melting ice caps and glaciers and rising sea levels can seriously disrupt many ecosystems and affect numerous species. For example, the giant panda feeds almost exclusively on bamboo. Bamboo is being threatened by global warming. Due to the dwindling of their food source, giant pandas are less able to adapt to a changing environment. The polar bear may become extinct due to global warming as the polar bears' habitat is destroyed. Sea turtles may become extinct as the rising sea levels destroy the beaches needed for egg laying. Even if the beaches are not destroyed, increasing temperatures affect the incubation process and the number of offspring being produced.

Human impacts

Humans are responsible for impacting the environment in such a way as to endanger or harm species that may even lead to extinction. Humans destroy habitats directly through deforestation and clearing land for agriculture, logging, mining, and urbanization. Humans also threaten or endanger species through overfishing and overhunting. Pollution can destroy a habitat, and if a species is unable to relocate, this can cause extinction. Introduction of an invasive species that introduces a new predator or competitor to the ecosystem can cause extinction. An example of human impacts leading to the extinction of a species is the case of the passenger pigeon. Millions of

Copyright © Mometrix Media. You have been licensed one copy of this document for personal use only. Any other reproduction or redistribution is strictly prohibited. All rights reserved.

passenger pigeons were killed for meat from around 1850 to 1880. Because passenger pigeons only laid one egg at a time, huge flocks were destroyed. The last passenger pigeon died in 1914.

> **Review Video:** Genetic vs. Environmental Traits
> Visit mometrix.com/academy and enter code: 750684

Interspecific competition

Interspecific competition is competition between individuals of different species for the same limited resources such as food, water, sunlight, and living space. This is especially threatening if the two species share a limiting resource and that resource is not in abundant supply. Interspecific competition can limit the population size of a species. With reduced population size, there is less genetic variation. The species may not be able to adapt to environmental changes. For example, firs and spruces compete for resources in coniferous forests. Cheetahs and lions compete for prey in savannas.

Copyright © Mometrix Media. You have been licensed one copy of this document for personal use only. Any other reproduction or redistribution is strictly prohibited. All rights reserved.

Biological Unity and Diversity and Life Processes

Importance and structural organization of cells

Cells are the basic structural units of all organisms. All organisms have a highly organized cellular structure. In single-celled organisms, that single cell contains all of the components necessary for life. In multicellular organisms, cells can become specialized. Different types of cells can have different functions. Life begins as a single cell whether by asexual or sexual reproduction. All cells contain DNA and RNA and can synthesize proteins. Each cell consists of nucleic acids, cytoplasm, and a cell membrane. Specialized organelles such as mitochondria and chloroplasts have specific functions within the cell.

Energy

All cells must obtain and use energy in order to grow, make repairs, and reproduce. Cells use energy to take in food, process that food, and eliminate wastes from this process. Cells obtain the energy they need by the breaking of bonds of molecules. Organisms differ in how they obtain food. Plants and other autotrophs produce energy through photosynthesis or chemosynthesis. Animals and other heterotrophs obtain their energy from consuming autotrophs or other heterotrophs. Cellular respiration is the process of converting nutrient molecules into energy.

Growth and reproduction

All organisms must be capable of growth and reproduction. Growth is necessary for multicellular organisms to develop and mature. Growth allows cells to be replaced or repaired. All cells eventually die. Without growth from cell division, tissues could not be maintained or repaired. Through mitosis, most cells routinely replace themselves with identical daughter cells. All organisms eventually die. Reproduction is necessary to increase the number of individuals in a population. Reproduction is either sexual by the joining of gametes or asexual by binary fission or some other related method. Not all organisms reproduce, but all must grow or they will die. Even single-celled organisms grow a small amount.

Adaptation to environment

Organisms must be able to adapt to their environment in order to thrive or survive. Individual organisms must be able to recognize stimuli in their surroundings and adapt quickly. For example, an individual euglena can sense light and respond by moving toward the light. Individual organisms must also be able to adapt to changes in the environment on a larger scale. For example, plants must be able to respond to the change in the length of the day to flower at the correct time. Populations must also be able to adapt to a changing environment. Evolution by natural selection is the process by which populations change over many generations. For example, wooly mammoths were unable to adapt to a warming climate and are now extinct, but many species of deer did adapt and are abundant today.

Structure, organization, modes of nutrition, and reproduction of animals

Animals are multicellular organism with eukaryotic cells that do not have cell walls surrounding their plasma membranes. Animals have several possible structural body forms. Animals can be relatively simple in structure such as sponges, which do not have a nervous system. Other animals are more complex with cells organized into tissues, and tissues organized into organs, and organs even further organized into systems. Invertebrates such as arthropods, nematodes, and annelids

Copyright © Mometrix Media. You have been licensed one copy of this document for personal use only. Any other reproduction or redistribution is strictly prohibited. All rights reserved.

have complex body systems. Vertebrates including fish, amphibians, reptiles, birds, and mammals are the most complex with detailed systems such as those with gills, air sacs, or lungs designed to exchange respiratory gases. All animals are heterotrophs and obtain their nutrition by consuming autotrophs or other heterotrophs. Most animals are motile, but some animals move their environment to bring food to them. All animals reproduce sexually at some point in their life cycle. Typically, this involves the union of a sperm and egg to produce a zygote.

> **Review Video: <u>Arthropoda</u>**
> Visit mometrix.com/academy and enter code: 523466

Characteristics of the major animal phyla

<u>Body planes</u>

Animals can exhibit bilateral symmetry, radial symmetry, or asymmetry. With bilateral symmetry, the organism can be cut in half along only one plane to produce two identical halves. Most animals, including all vertebrates such as mammals, birds, reptiles, amphibians, and fish, exhibit bilateral symmetry. Many invertebrates including arthropods and crustaceans also exhibit bilateral symmetry. With radial symmetry, the organism can be cut in half along several planes to produce two identical halves. Starfish, sea urchins, and jellyfish exhibit radial symmetry. With asymmetry, the organism exhibits no symmetry. Very few organisms in the animal phyla exhibit asymmetry, but a few species of sponges are asymmetrical.

<u>Body cavities</u>

Animals can be grouped based on their types of body cavities. A coelom is a fluid-filled body cavity between the alimentary canal and the body wall. The three body plans based on the formation of the coelom are acoelomates, pseudocoelomates, and coelomates. Acoelomates do not have body cavities. Pseudocoelomates have a body cavity called a pseudocoelom. Pseudocoeloms are not considered true coeloms. Pseudocoeloms are located between mesoderm and endoderm instead of actually in the mesoderm as in a true coelom. Coelomates have a true coelom located within the mesoderm. Simple or primitive animals such as sponges, jellyfish, sea anemones, hydras, flatworms, and ribbon worms are acoelomates. Pseudocoelomates include roundworms and rotifers. Most animals including arthropods, mollusks, annelids, echinoderms, and chordates are coelomates.

<u>Modes of reproduction</u>

Animals can reproduce sexually or asexually. Most animals reproduce sexually. In sexual reproduction, males and females have different reproductive organs that produce gametes. Males have testes that produce sperm, and females have ovaries that produce eggs. During fertilization, a sperm cell unites with an egg cell, forming a zygote. Fertilization can occur internally such as in most mammals and birds or externally such as aquatic animals such as fish and frogs. The zygote undergoes cell division, which develops into an embryo and eventually develops into an adult organism. Some embryos develop in eggs such as in fish, amphibians, reptiles, and birds. Some mammals are oviparous and lay eggs. Most mammals are viviparous and have a uterus in which the embryo develops. Some mammals are marsupials and give birth to an immature fetus that finishes developing in a pouch. Some animals reproduce asexually. For example, hydras reproduce by budding, and starfish and planarians can reproduce by fragmentation and regeneration. Some fish, frogs, and insects reproduce by parthenogenesis.

<u>Modes of temperature regulation</u>

Animals can be classified as either homeotherms or poikilotherms. Homeotherms, also called warm-blooded animals or endotherms, maintain a constant body temperature regardless of the

- 70 -

Copyright © Mometrix Media. You have been licensed one copy of this document for personal use only. Any other reproduction or redistribution is strictly prohibited. All rights reserved.

temperature of the environment. Homeotherms such as mammals and birds have a high metabolic rate because much energy is needed to maintain the constant temperature. Poikilotherms, also called cold-blooded animals or ectotherms, do not maintain a constant body temperature. Their body temperature fluctuates with the temperature of the environment. Poikilotherms such as arthropods, fish, amphibians, and reptiles have metabolic rates that fluctuate with their body temperature.

> **Review Video: Basic Characteristics of Organisms**
> Visit mometrix.com/academy and enter code: 314694

Cells

Cells are the basic structural units of all living things. Cells are composed of various molecules including proteins, carbohydrates, lipids, and nucleic acids. All animal cells are eukaryotic and have a nucleus, cytoplasm, and a cell membrane. Organelles include mitochondria, ribosomes, endoplasmic reticulum, Golgi apparatuses, and vacuoles. Specialized cells are numerous, including but not limited to various muscle cells, nerve cells, epithelial cells, bone cells, blood cells, and cartilage cells. Cells are grouped to together in tissues to perform specific functions.

Organizational hierarchy within multicellular organisms

Cells are the smallest living units of organisms. Tissues are groups of cells that work together to perform a specific function. Organs are groups of tissues that work together to perform a specific function. Organ systems are groups of organs that work together to perform a specific function. An organism is an individual that contains several body systems.

Tissues

Tissues are groups of cells that work together to perform a specific function. Tissues can be grouped into four broad categories: muscle tissue, nerve tissue, epithelial tissue, and connective tissue. Muscle tissue is involved in body movement. Muscle tissues can be composed of skeletal muscle cells, cardiac muscle cells, or smooth muscle cells. Skeletal muscles include the muscles commonly called biceps, triceps, hamstrings, and quadriceps. Cardiac muscle tissue is found only in the heart. Smooth muscle tissue provides tension in the blood vessels, controls pupil dilation, and aids in peristalsis. Nerve tissue is located in the brain, spinal cord, and nerves. Epithelial tissue makes up the layers of the skin and various membranes. Connective tissues include bone tissue, cartilage, tendons, ligaments, fat, blood, and lymph. Tissues are grouped together as organs to perform specific functions.

Organs and organ systems

Organs are groups of tissues that work together to perform specific functions. Organ systems are groups of organs that work together to perform specific functions. Complex animals have several organs that are grouped together in multiple systems. In mammals, there are 11 major organ systems: integumentary system, respiratory system, cardiovascular system, endocrine system, nervous system, immune system, digestive system, excretory system, muscular system, skeletal system, and reproductive system.

Cardiovascular system

The main functions of the cardiovascular system are gas exchange, the delivery of nutrients and hormones, and waste removal. The cardiovascular system consists primarily of the heart, blood,

- 71 -

Copyright © Mometrix Media. You have been licensed one copy of this document for personal use only. Any other reproduction or redistribution is strictly prohibited. All rights reserved.

and blood vessels. The heart is a pump that pushes blood through the arteries. Arteries are blood vessels that carry blood away from the heart, and veins are blood vessels that carry blood back to the heart. The exchange of materials between blood and cells occur in the capillaries, which are the smallest of the blood vessels. All vertebrates and a few invertebrates including annelids, squids, and octopuses have a closed circulatory system. Mammals, birds and crocodilians have a four-chambered heart. Most amphibians and reptiles have a three-chambered heart. Fish have only a two-chambered heart. Arthropods and most mollusks have open circulatory systems. Many invertebrates do not have a cardiovascular system. For example, echinoderms have a water vascular system.

Respiratory system

The function of the respiratory system is to move air in and out of the body in order to facilitate the exchange of oxygen and carbon dioxide. The respiratory system consists of the nasal passages, pharynx, larynx, trachea, bronchial tubes, lungs, and diaphragm. Bronchial tubes branch into bronchioles, which end in clusters of alveoli. The alveoli are tiny sacs inside the lungs where gas exchange takes place. When the diaphragm contracts, the volume of the chest increases, which reduces the pressure in the lungs. Then, air is inhaled through the nose or mouth and passes through the pharynx, larynx, trachea, and bronchial tubes into the lungs. When the diaphragm relaxes, the volume in the chest cavity decreases, forcing the air out of the lungs.

Reproductive system

The main function of the reproductive system is to propagate the species. Most animals reproduce sexually at some point in their life cycle. Typically, this involves the union of a sperm and egg to produce a zygote. In complex animals, the female reproductive system includes one or more ovaries, which produce the egg cell. The male reproductive system includes one or more testes, which produce the sperm.

Internal and external fertilization

Eggs may be fertilized internally or externally. In internal fertilization in mammals, the sperm unites with the egg in the oviduct. In mammals, the zygote begins to divide, and the blastula implants in the uterus. In birds, after the egg is fertilized, albumen, membranes, and egg shell are added. Reptiles lay amniotic eggs covered by a leathery shell. Amphibians and most fish fertilize eggs externally. But some fish give birth to live young.

Invertebrates

Most invertebrates reproduce sexually. Invertebrates may have separate sexes or be hermaphroditic, in which the organisms produces sperm and eggs either at the same time or separately at some time in their life cycle. Many invertebrates such as insects also have complex reproductive systems. Some invertebrates reproduce asexually by budding, fragmentation, or parthenogenesis.

Digestive system

The main function of the digestive system is to process the food that is consumed by the animal. This includes mechanical and chemical processing. Depending on the animal, mechanical processes can happen in various ways. Mammals have teeth to chew their food. Saliva is secreted, which contains enzymes to begin the breakdown of starches. Many animals such as birds, earthworms, crocodilians, and crustaceans have a gizzard or gizzard-like organ that grinds the food. Many animals such as mammals, birds, reptiles, amphibians, and fish have a stomach that stores and

Copyright © Mometrix Media. You have been licensed one copy of this document for personal use only. Any other reproduction or redistribution is strictly prohibited. All rights reserved.

absorbs food. Gastric juice containing enzymes and hydrochloric acid is mixed with the food. The intestine or intestines absorb nutrients and reabsorb water from the undigested material. Many animals have a liver, gallbladder, and pancreas, which aid in digestion of proteins and fats although not being part of the muscular tube through which the waste passes. Undigested wasted are eliminated from the body through an anus or cloaca.

Excretory system

All animals have some type of excretory system that has the main function of metabolizing food and eliminating metabolic wastes. In complex animals such as mammals, the excretory system consists of the kidneys, ureters, urinary bladder, and urethra. Urea and other toxic wastes must be eliminated from the body. The kidneys constantly filter the blood. The nephron is the working unit of the kidney. Each nephron functions like a tiny filter. Nephrons not only filter the blood, but they also facilitate reabsorption and secretion. Basically, the glomerulus filters the blood. Water and dissolved materials such as glucose and amino acids pass on into the Bowman's capsule. Depending on concentration gradients, water and dissolved materials can pass back into the blood primarily through the proximal convoluted tubule. Additional water can be removed at the loop of Henle. Antidiuretic hormone regulates the water that is lost or reabsorbed. Urine passes from the kidneys through the ureters to the urinary bladder where it is stored before it is expelled from the body through the urethra.

Kidneys

The kidneys are involved in blood filtration, pH balance, and the reabsorption of nutrients to maintain proper blood volume and ion balance. The nephron is the working unit of the kidney. The parts of the nephron include the glomerulus, Bowman's capsule, and loop of Henle. Filtration takes place in the nephron's glomerulus. Water and dissolved materials such as glucose and amino acids pass on into the Bowman's capsule. Depending on concentration gradients, water and dissolved materials can pass back into the blood primarily through the proximal convoluted tubule. Reabsorption and water removal occurs in the loop of Henle and the conducting duct. Urine and other nitrogenous wastes pass from the kidneys to the bladders and are expelled.

Nervous system

All animals except sponges have a nervous system. The main function of the nervous system is to coordinate the activities of the body. The nervous system consists of the brain, spinal cord, peripheral nerves, and sense organs. Sense organs such as the ears, eyes, nose, taste buds, and pressure receptors receive stimuli from the environment and relay that information through nerves and the spinal cord to the brain where the information is processed. The brain sends signals through the spinal cord and peripheral nerves to the organs and muscles. The autonomic nervous system controls all routine body functions by the sympathetic and parasympathetic divisions. Reflexes, which are also part of the nervous system, may involve only a few nerve cells and bypass the brain when an immediate response is necessary.

Endocrine system

The endocrine system consists of several ductless glands, which secrete hormones directly into the bloodstream. The pituitary gland is the master gland, which controls the functions of the other glands. The pituitary gland regulates skeletal growth and the development of the reproductive organs. The pineal gland regulates sleep cycles. The thyroid gland regulates metabolism and helps regulate the calcium level in the blood. The parathyroid glands also help regulate the blood calcium level. The adrenal glands secrete the emergency hormone epinephrine, stimulate body repairs, and

Copyright © Mometrix Media. You have been licensed one copy of this document for personal use only. Any other reproduction or redistribution is strictly prohibited. All rights reserved.

regulate sodium and potassium levels in the blood. The islets of Langerhans located in the pancreas secrete insulin and glucagon to regulate the blood sugar level. In females, ovaries produce estrogen, which stimulates sexual development, and progesterone, which functions during pregnancy. In males, the testes secrete testosterone, which stimulates sexual development and sperm production.

Immune system

The immune system in animals defends the body against infection and disease. The immune system can be divided into two broad categories: innate immunity and adaptive immunity. Innate immunity includes the skin and mucous membranes, which provide a physical barrier to prevent pathogens from entering the body. Special chemicals including enzymes and proteins in mucus, tears, sweat, and stomach juices destroy pathogens. Numerous white blood cells such as neutrophils and macrophages protect the body from invading pathogens. Adaptive immunity involves the body responding to a specific antigen. Typically, B-lymphocytes or B cells produce antibodies against a specific antigen, and T-lymphocytes or T-cells take special roles as helpers, regulators, or killers. Some T-cells function as memory cells.

> **Review Video: Antibodies**
> Visit mometrix.com/academy and enter code: 549715

Maintenance of homeostasis in organisms

Role of feedback mechanisms

Feedback mechanisms play a major role in homeostasis in organisms. Each feedback mechanism consists of receptors, an integrator, and effectors. Receptors such as mechanoreceptors or thermoreceptors in the skin detect the stimuli. The integrator such as the brain or spinal cord receives the information concerning the stimuli and sends out signals to other parts of the body. The effectors such as muscles or glands respond to the stimulus. Basically, the receptors receive the stimuli and notify the integrator, which signals the effectors to respond. Feedback mechanisms can be negative or positive. Negative-feedback mechanisms are mechanisms that provide a decrease in response with an increase in stimulus that inhibits the stimulus, which in turn decreases the response. Positive-feedback mechanisms are mechanisms that provide an increase in response with an increase in stimulus, which actually increases the stimulus, which in turn increases the response.

Role of hypothalamus

The hypothalamus plays a major role in the homoeostasis of vertebrates. Homeostasis is regulation of internal chemistry to maintain a constant internal environment. The hypothalamus is the central portion of the brain just above the brainstem, which is linked to the endocrine system through the pituitary gland. The hypothalamus releases special hormones that influence the secretion of pituitary hormones. The hypothalamus regulates the fundamental physiological state by controlling body temperature, hunger, thirst, sleep, behaviors related to attachment, sexual development, fight-or-flight stress response, and circadian rhythms.

Role of endocrine system and hormones

All vertebrates have an endocrine system that consists of numerous ductless glands that produce hormones that help coordinate many functions of the body. Hormones are signaling molecules that are received by receptors. Many hormones are secreted in response to signals from the pituitary gland and hypothalamus gland. Other hormones are secreted in response to signals from inside the body. Hormones can consist of amino acids, proteins, or lipid molecules such as steroid hormones. Hormones can affect target cells, which have the correct receptor that is able to bind to that

- 74 -

Copyright © Mometrix Media. You have been licensed one copy of this document for personal use only. Any other reproduction or redistribution is strictly prohibited. All rights reserved.

particular hormone. Most cells have receptors for more than one type of hormone. Hormones are distributed to the target cells in the blood by the cardiovascular system. Hormones incorporate feedback mechanisms to help the body maintain homeostasis.

Role of antidiuretic hormone

Antidiuretic hormone (ADH) helps maintain homeostasis in vertebrates. ADH is produced by the posterior pituitary gland, and it regulates the reabsorption of water in the kidneys and concentrates the urine. The stimulus in this feedback mechanism is a drop in blood volume due to water loss. This signal is picked up by the hypothalamus, which signals the pituitary gland to secrete ADH. ADH is carried by the cardiovascular system to the nephrons in the kidneys signaling them to reabsorb more water and send less out as waste. As more water is reabsorbed, the blood volume increases, which is monitored by the hypothalamus. As the blood volume reaches the set point, the hypothalamus signals for a decrease in the secretion of ADH, and the cycle continues.

Role of insulin and glucagon

Insulin and glucagon are hormones that help maintain the glucose concentration in the blood. Insulin and glucagon are secreted by the clumps of endocrine cells called the pancreatic islets that are located in the pancreas. Insulin and glucagon work together to maintain the blood glucose level. Insulin stimulates cells to remove glucose from the blood. Glucagon stimulates the liver to convert glycogen to glucose. After eating, glucose levels increase in the blood. This stimulus signals the pancreas to stop the secretion of glucagon and to start secreting insulin. Cells respond to the insulin and remove glucose from the blood, lowering the level of glucose in the blood. Later, after eating, the level of glucose in the blood decreases further. This stimulus signals the pancreas to secrete glucagon and decrease the secretion of insulin. In response to the stimulus, the liver converts glycogen to glucose, and the level of glucose in the blood rises. When the individual eats, the cycle begins again.

Thermoregulation

Animals exhibit many adaptations that help them achieve homeostasis, or a stable internal environment. Some of these adaptions are behavioral. Most organisms exhibit some type of behavioral thermoregulation. Thermoregulation is the ability to keep the body temperature within certain boundaries. The type of behavioral thermoregulation depends on whether the animal is an endotherm or an ectotherm. Ectotherms are "cold-blooded," and their body temperature changes with their external environment. To regulate their temperature, ectotherms often move to an appropriate location. Fish move to warmer waters. Animals will climb to higher grounds. Diurnal ectotherms such as reptiles often bask in the sun to increase their body temperatures. Butterflies are heliotherms in that they derive nearly all of their heat from basking in the sun. Endotherms are "warm-blooded" and maintain a stable body temperature by internal means. However, many animals that live in hot environments have adapted to the nocturnal lifestyle. Desert animals are often nocturnal to escape high daytime temperatures. Other nocturnal animals sleep during the day in underground burrows or dens. Birds can spread their wings to capture heat from the sun.

Gamete formation

Gametogenesis is the formation of gametes. Gametes are reproductive cells. Gametes are produced by meiosis. Meiosis is a special type of cell division that consists of two consecutive mitotic divisions referred to as meiosis I and meiosis II. Meiosis I is a reduction division in which a diploid cell is reduced to two haploid daughter cells that contain only one of each pair of homologous chromosomes. During meiosis II, those haploid cells are further divided to form four haploid cells. Spermatogenesis in males produces four viable sperm cells from each complete cycle of meiosis.

Copyright © Mometrix Media. You have been licensed one copy of this document for personal use only. Any other reproduction or redistribution is strictly prohibited. All rights reserved.

Oogenesis produces four daughter cells, but only one is a viable egg and the other three are polar bodies.

Fertilization

Fertilization is the union of a sperm cell and an egg cell to produce a zygote. Many sperm may bind to an egg, but only one joins with the egg and injects its nuclei into the egg. Fertilization can be external or internal. External fertilization takes place outside of the female's body. For example, many fish, amphibians, crustaceans, mollusks, and corals reproduce externally by spawning or releasing gametes into the water simultaneously or right after each other. Reptiles and birds reproduce by internal fertilization. All mammals except monotremes (e.g. platypus) reproduce by internal fertilization.

Embryonic development

Embryonic development in animals is typically divided into four stages: cleavage, patterning, differentiation, and growth. Cleavage occurs immediately after fertilization when the large single-celled zygote immediately begins to divide into smaller and smaller cells without an increase in mass. A hollow ball of cells forms a blastula. Next, during patterning, gastrulation occurs. During gastrulation, the cells are organized into three primary germ layers: ectoderm, mesoderm, and endoderm. Then, the cells in these layers differentiate into special tissues and organs. For example, the nervous system develops from the ectoderm. The muscular system develops from the mesoderm. Much of the digestive system develops from the endoderm. The final stage of embryonic development is growth and further tissue specialization. The embryo continues to grow until ready for hatching or birth.

Postnatal growth

Postnatal growth occurs from hatching or birth until death. The length of the postnatal growth depends on the species. Elephants can live 70 years, but mice only about 4 years. Right after animals are hatched or born, they go through a period of rapid growth and development. In vertebrates, bones lengthen, muscles grow in bulk, and fat is deposited. At maturity, bones stop growing in length, but bones can grow in width and repair themselves throughout the animal's lifetime, and muscle deposition slows down. Fat cells continue to increase and decrease in size throughout the animal's life. Growth is controlled by genetics but is also influenced by nutrition and disease. Most animals are sexually mature in less than two years and can produce offspring.

Viruses

Viruses are nonliving, infectious particles that act as parasites in living organisms. Viruses are acellular, which means that they lack cell structure. Viruses cannot reproduce outside of living cells. The structure of a virus is a core of a nucleic acid, which may be either DNA or RNA, surrounded by a protein coat or capsid. In some viruses, the capsid may be surrounded by a lipid membrane or envelope. Viruses can contain up to 500 genes. Viruses have various shapes and usually are too small to be seen without the aid of an electron microscope. Viruses can infect plants, animals, fungi, protists, and bacteria. Viruses can attack only specific types of cells that have specific receptors on their surfaces. Viruses do not divide or reproduce like living cells. Viruses are replicated by the machinery of the host cell. The nucleic acid of the virus takes control of the host cell's metabolic pathways to make copies of itself. The host cell usually bursts to release these copies.

Copyright © Mometrix Media. You have been licensed one copy of this document for personal use only. Any other reproduction or redistribution is strictly prohibited. All rights reserved.

Bacteria

Bacteria are small, prokaryotic, single-celled organisms. Bacteria have a circular loop of DNA (plasmid) that is not contained within a nuclear membrane. Bacterial ribosomes are not bound to endoplasmic reticulum, as in eukaryotes. A cell wall containing peptidoglycan surrounds the bacterial plasma membrane. Some bacteria such as pathogens are further encased in gel-like capsules. Bacteria can be autotrophs or heterotrophs. Some bacteria heterotrophs are saprophytes that function as decomposers in ecosystems, and some are pathogens. Many types of bacteria share commensal or mutualistic relationships with other organisms. Most bacteria reproduce asexually by binary fission. Two identical daughter cells are produced from one parent cell. Some bacteria can transfer genetic material to other bacteria through a process called conjugation. Some bacteria can incorporate DNA from the environment in a process called transformation.

Protists

Protists are small, eukaryotic, single-celled organisms. Although protists are small, they are much larger than prokaryotic bacteria. Protists have three general forms, which include plantlike protists, animal-like protists, and fungus-like protists. Plantlike protists are algae that contain chlorophyll and perform photosynthesis. Animal-like protists are protozoa with no cell walls that typically lack chlorophyll and are grouped by their method of locomotion. Fungus-like protists, which do not have chitin in their cell walls, are generally grouped as either slime molds or water molds. Protists may be autotrophic or heterotrophic. Autotrophic protists include many species of algae. Heterotrophic protists include parasitic, commensalistic, and mutualistic protozoa. Slime molds are heterotrophic fungus-like protists, which consume microorganisms. Some protists reproduce sexually, but most reproduce asexually by binary fission. Some reproduce asexually by spores. Some reproduce by alternation of generations and require two hosts in their life cycle.

Fungi

Fungi are nonmotile organisms with eukaryotic cells containing chitin in their cell walls. Most fungi are multicellular, but a few including yeast are unicellular. Fungi have multicellular filaments called hyphae that are grouped together in mycelia. Fungi do not perform photosynthesis. All fungi are heterotrophs. Fungi can be parasitic, mutualistic or free living. Free-living fungi include mushrooms and toadstools. Parasitic fungi include fungi responsible for ringworm and athlete's foot. Mycorrhizae are mutualistic fungi that live in or near plant roots increasing the roots' surface area of absorption. Almost all fungi reproduce asexually by spores, but most fungi also have a sexual phase in the production of spores. Some fungi reproduce by budding or fragmentation.

> **Review Video: Feeding Among Heterotrophs**
> Visit mometrix.com/academy and enter code: 836017
>
> **Review Video: Kingdom Fungi**
> Visit mometrix.com/academy and enter code: 315081

Plants

Plants are multicellular organisms with eukaryotic cells containing cellulose in their cell walls. Plant cells have chlorophyll and perform photosynthesis. Plants can be vascular or nonvascular. Vascular plants have true leaves, stems, and roots that contain xylem and phloem. Nonvascular plants lack true leaves, stems and roots and do not have any true vascular tissue but instead rely on diffusion and osmosis for most transport of materials. Almost all plants are autotrophic, relying on

Copyright © Mometrix Media. You have been licensed one copy of this document for personal use only. Any other reproduction or redistribution is strictly prohibited. All rights reserved.

photosynthesis for food. A small number do not have chlorophyll and are parasitic, but these are extremely rare. Plants can reproduce sexually or asexually. Many plants reproduce by seeds produced in the fruits of the plants. Some plants reproduce by seeds on cones. Ferns reproduce by spores. Some plants can reproduce asexually by vegetative reproduction.

Review Video: Kingdom Plantae
Visit mometrix.com/academy and enter code: 710084

Vascular and nonvascular plants

Vascular plants, also referred to as tracheophytes, have dermal tissue, meristematic tissue, ground tissues, and vascular tissues. Nonvascular plants, also referred to a bryophytes, do not have the vascular tissue xylem and phloem. Vascular plants can grow very tall, whereas nonvascular plants are short and close to the ground. Vascular plants can be found in dry regions, but nonvascular plants typically grow near or in moist areas. Vascular plants have leaves, roots, and stems, but nonvascular plants have leaflike, rootlike, and stemlike structures that do not have true vascular tissue. Vascular plants include angiosperms, gymnosperms, and ferns. Nonvascular plants include mosses and liverworts.

Flowering versus nonflowering plants

Angiosperms and gymnosperms are both vascular plants. Angiosperms are flowering plants, and gymnosperms are nonflowering plants. Angiosperms reproduce by seeds that are enclosed in an ovary, usually in a fruit. Angiosperms can be further classified as either monocots or dicots. Gymnosperms reproduce by unenclosed or "naked" seeds on scales, leaves, or cones. Angiosperms include grasses, garden flowers, vegetables, and broadleaf trees such as maples, birches, elms, and oaks. Gymnosperms include conifers such as pines, spruces, cedars, and redwoods.

Review Video: Fruits in Flowering Plants
Visit mometrix.com/academy and enter code: 867090

Monocots and dicots

Angiosperms can be classified as either monocots or dicots. The seeds of monocots have one cotyledon, and the seeds of dicots have two cotyledons. The flowers of monocots have petals in multiples of three, and the flowers of dicots have petals in multiples of four or five. The leaves of monocots are slender with parallel veins, and the leaves of dicots are broad and flat with branching veins. The vascular bundles in monocots are distributed throughout the stem. The vascular bundles in dicots are arranged in rings. Monocots have a fibrous root system, and dicots have a taproot system.

Plant dermal tissue

Plant dermal tissue consists of the epidermis and the dermis. The epidermis is usually a single layer of cells that covers younger plants. The epidermis protects the plant by secreting the cuticle, which is a waxy substance that helps prevent water loss and infections. The epidermis in leaves has tiny pores called stomata. Guard cells in the epidermis control the opening and closing of the stomata. The epidermis usually does not have chloroplasts. The epidermis may be replaced by periderm in older plants. The periderm is also referred to as bark. The layers of the periderm are cork cells or phellem, phelloderm, and cork cambium or phellogen. Cork is the outer layer of the periderm and consists of nonliving cells. The periderm protects the plant and provides insulation.

Copyright © Mometrix Media. You have been licensed one copy of this document for personal use only. Any other reproduction or redistribution is strictly prohibited. All rights reserved.

Plant vascular tissue

The two major types of plant vascular tissue are xylem and phloem. Xylem and phloem are bound together in vascular bundles. A meristem called vascular cambium is located between the xylem and phloem and produces new xylem and phloem. Xylem is made up of tracheids and vessel elements. All vascular plants contain tracheids, but only angiosperms contain vessel elements. Xylem provides support and conducts water and dissolved minerals from the root and upward throughout the plant by transpirational pull and root pressure. In woody plants, xylem is commonly referred to as wood. Phloem is made up of companion cells and sieve-tube cells. Phloem conducts nutrients including sucrose produced during photosynthesis and organic materials throughout the plant. By active transport, the companion vessels move glucose in and out of the sieve-tube cells.

Plant ground tissue

The three major types of ground tissue are parenchyma tissue, collenchyma tissue, and sclerenchyma tissue. Most ground tissue is made up of parenchyma. Parenchyma is formed by parenchyma cells, and it provides photosynthesis, food storage, and tissue repair. The soft "filler" tissues in plants are usually parenchyma. The mesophyll in leaves is parenchyma tissue. Collenchyma is made of collenchyma cells and provides support in roots, stems, and petioles. Sclerenchyma tissue is made of sclereid cells, which are more rigid than the collenchyma cells, and provides rigid support and protection. Plant sclerenchyma tissue may contain cellulose or lignin. Fabrics such as jute, hemp, and flax are made of sclerenchyma tissue.

Plant meristematic tissue

Meristems or meristematic tissues are the regions of plant growth. The cells in meristems are undifferentiated and always remain totipotent, which means they can always develop into any type of special tissue. Meristem cells produce all the new cells in a plant and regenerate damaged parts. Cells of meristems reproduce asexually through mitosis or cell division that is regulated by hormones. The two types of meristems are lateral meristems and apical meristems. Primary growth occurs at apical meristems. Roots and shoots have meristem tissue at their tips and can grow in length. Primary meristems include the protoderm, which produces epidermis; the procambium, which produces cambium; xylem and phloem; and the ground meristem, which produces ground tissue including parenchyma. Secondary growth occurs at the lateral or secondary meristems. Secondary meristems include the vascular cambium and cork cambium. Secondary growth causes an increase in diameter.

Flowers

The primary function of flowers is to produce seeds for reproduction of the plant. Flowers have a pedicel or stalk with a receptacle or enlarged upper portion, which holds the developing seeds. Flowers also can have sepals and petals. Sepals are leaflike structures and protect the bud. Petals, which are collectively called the corolla, help to attract pollinators. Plants can have stamens, pistils, or both depending on the type of plant. The stamen consists of the anther and filament. The anther

Copyright © Mometrix Media. You have been licensed one copy of this document for personal use only. Any other reproduction or redistribution is strictly prohibited. All rights reserved.

produces the pollen, which produces the sperm cells. The pistil consists of the stigma, style, and ovary. The ovary contains the ovules, which house the egg cells.

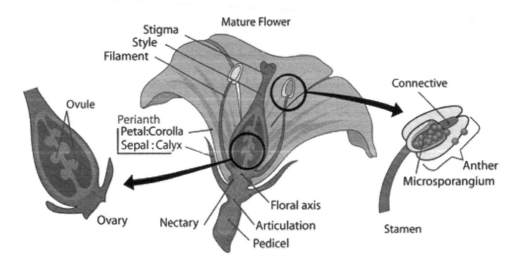

Stems

Plants can have either woody or nonwoody (herbaceous) stems. The stem is divided into nodes and internodes. Buds are located at the nodes and may develop into leaves, roots, flowers, cones, or more stems. Stems consist of dermal tissue, ground tissue, and vascular tissue. Dicot stems have vascular bundles distributed through the stem. Monocots have rings of vascular bundles. Stems have four main functions: (1) they provide support to leaves, flowers, and fruits; (2) they transport materials in the xylem and phloem; (3) they store food; and (4) they have meristems, which provide all of the new cells for the plant.

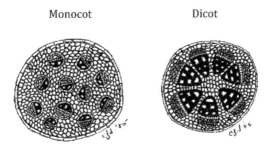

Leaves

The primary function of a leaf is to manufacture food through photosynthesis. The leaf consists of a flat portion called the blade and a stalk called the petiole. The edge of the leaf is called the margin and can be entire, toothed, or lobed. Veins transport food and water and make up the skeleton of the leaf. The large central vein is called the midrib. The blade has an upper and lower epidermis. The epidermis is covered by a protective cuticle. The lower epidermis contains many stomata, which are pores that allow air to enter and leave the leaf. Stomata also regulate transpiration. The middle portion of the leaf is called the mesophyll. The mesophyll consists of the palisade mesophyll

Copyright © Mometrix Media. You have been licensed one copy of this document for personal use only. Any other reproduction or redistribution is strictly prohibited. All rights reserved.

and the spongy mesophyll. Most photosynthesis occurs in chloroplasts located in the palisade mesophyll.

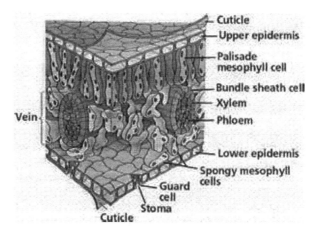

Roots

The primary functions of roots are to anchor the plant, absorb materials, and store food. The two basic types of root systems are taproot systems and fibrous root systems. Taproot systems have a primary root with many smaller secondary roots. Fibrous root systems, which lack a primary root, consist of a mass of many small secondary roots. The root has three main regions: the area of maturation, the area of elongation, and the area of cell division or the meristematic region. The root is covered by an epidermal cell, some of which develops into root hairs. Root hairs absorb water and minerals by osmosis, and capillary action helps move the water upward through the roots to the rest of the plant. The center of the root is the vascular cylinder, which contains the xylem and phloem. The vascular cylinder is surrounded by the cortex where the food is stored. Primary growth occurs at the root tip. Secondary growth occurs at the vascular cambium located between the xylem and phloem.

Pollination strategies

Pollination is the transfer of pollen from the anther of the stamen to the stigma of the pistil on the same plant or on a different plant. Pollinators can be either abiotic (not derived from a living organism) or biotic (derived from a living organism). Abiotic pollinators include wind and water. Approximately 20% of pollination occurs by abiotic pollinators. For example, grasses are typically pollinated by wind, and aquatic plants are typically pollinated by water. Biotic pollinators include insects, birds, mammals, and occasionally reptiles. Most biotic pollinators are insects. Many plants have colored petals and strong scents, which attract insects. Pollen rubs off on the insects and is transferred as they move from plant to plant.

Seed dispersal methods

Methods of seed dispersal can be abiotic or biotic. Methods of seed dispersal include gravity, wind, water, and animals. Some plants produce seeds in fruits that get eaten by animals and then are distributed to new locations in the animals' waste. Some seeds (e.g. dandelions) have structures to aid in dispersal by wind. Some seeds have barbs that get caught in animal hair or bird feathers and are then carried to new locations by the animals. Some animals bury seeds for food storage but do not return for the seeds. The seeds of aquatic plants can be dispersed by water. The seeds of plants near rivers, streams, lakes, and beaches (e.g. coconuts) are often dispersed by water. Some plants,

Copyright © Mometrix Media. You have been licensed one copy of this document for personal use only. Any other reproduction or redistribution is strictly prohibited. All rights reserved.

in a method called mechanical dispersal, can propel or shoot their seeds away from them even up to several feet. Touch-me-nots and violets can reproduce by mechanical dispersal.

Alternation of generations

Alternation of generations, also referred to as metagenesis, contains both a sexual phase and an asexual phase in the life cycle of the plant. Mosses and ferns reproduce by alternation of generations: the sexual phase is called the gametophyte, and the asexual phase is called the sporophyte. During the sexual phase, a sperm fertilizes an egg to form a zygote. By mitosis, the zygote develops into the sporophyte. The sporangia in the sori of the sporophyte produce the spores through meiosis. The spores germinate and by mitosis produce the gametophyte.

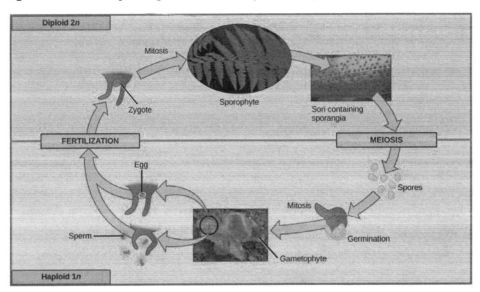

Obtaining and transporting water and inorganic nutrients

Inorganic nutrients (4) and water (5) enter plants through the root hair and travel to the xylem. Once the water, minerals, and salts have crossed the endodermis, they must be moved upward through the xylem by water uptake. Most of a plant's water is lost through the stomata (3) by transpiration. This loss is necessary to provide the tension needed to pull the water and nutrients up through the xylem. In order to maintain the remaining water that is necessary for the functioning of the plant, guard cells (2) control the stomata. Whether an individual stoma is closed or open is controlled by two guard cells. When the guard cells lose water and become flaccid, they collapse together, closing the stoma. When the guard cells swell with water and become turgid, they move apart, opening the stoma.

- 82 -

Copyright © Mometrix Media. You have been licensed one copy of this document for personal use only. Any other reproduction or redistribution is strictly prohibited. All rights reserved.

<u>Use of roots</u>

Plant roots have numerous root hairs that absorb water and inorganic nutrients such as minerals and salts. Root hairs are thin, hairlike outgrowths of the root's epidermal cells that exponentially increase the root's surface area. Water molecules cross the cell membranes of the root hairs by osmosis and then travel on to the vascular cylinder. Inorganic nutrients are transported across the cell membranes of the root endodermis by active transport. The endodermis is a single layer of cells that the water and nutrients must pass through by osmosis or active transport. Casparian strips, which are waxy waterproof deposits, line the channels between the cells of the endodermis to prevent crossing there. Water passes through by osmosis, but mineral uptake is controlled by transport proteins.

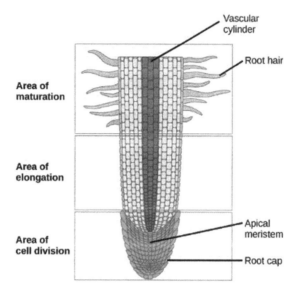

<u>Use of xylem</u>

The xylem contains dead, water-conducting cells called tracheids and vessels. The movement of water upward through the tracheids and vessels is explained by the cohesion-tension theory. First, water is lost through evaporation of the plant's surface through transpiration. This can occur at any surface exposed to air but is mainly through the stomata in the epidermis. This transpiration puts the water inside the xylem in a state of tension. Because water is cohesive due to the strong hydrogen bonds between molecules, the water is pulled up the xylem as long as the water is transpiring.

Glucose produced during photosynthesis

Plants produce glucose during photosynthesis. That glucose then enters reactions to form sucrose, starch, and cellulose. Glucose is a simple carbohydrate or monosaccharide. Plants do not transport glucose molecules. Instead, the glucose is joined to a fructose to form a sucrose, which is transported in sap. Sucrose is a disaccharide. Glucose and sucrose are simple carbohydrates. Starches and cellulose are long chains of glucose molecules called polysaccharides. Plants store glucose as starch, and plants use cellulose for rigidity in their cell walls. Both starch and cellulose are complex carbohydrates.

Use of phloem to transport products of photosynthesis

The movement of sugars and other materials from the leaves to other tissues throughout the plants is called translocation. Nutrients are translocated from sources (areas with excess sugars) such as

Copyright © Mometrix Media. You have been licensed one copy of this document for personal use only. Any other reproduction or redistribution is strictly prohibited. All rights reserved.

mature leaves to sinks (areas where sugars are needed) such as flowers, fruits, developing leaves, and roots. Phloem vessels are found in the vascular bundles along with the xylem. Phloem contains conducting cells called sieve elements, which are connected end to end in sieve tubes. Sieve tubes carry sap from sugar sources to sugar sinks. Phloem sap contains mostly sucrose dissolved in water. The sap can also contain proteins, amino acids, and hormones. Some plants transport sugar alcohols. Loading the sugar into the sieve tubes causes water to enter the tubes by osmosis, creating a higher hydrostatic pressure at the source end of the tube. Sugar is removed from the sieve tube at the sink end, and water again follows by osmosis lowering the pressure. This process is referred to as the pressure-flow mechanism.

Copyright © Mometrix Media. You have been licensed one copy of this document for personal use only. Any other reproduction or redistribution is strictly prohibited. All rights reserved.

Human Biology

Structure of the heart

The heart is a muscular pump that is enclosed in a tough white sac called the pericardium. The heart consists of four chambers: two upper chambers known as the atria and two lower chambers known as the ventricles. The left and right sides of the heart are separated by a thick wall called the septum. Atrioventricular valves lie on each side of the heart between each atria and ventricle. The bicuspid (mitral) valve lies on the left side, and the tricuspid valve lies on the right side. The semilunar valves are located at the exits of the ventricles. The aortic semilunar valve is located at the exit of the left ventricle to the aorta. The pulmonary semilunar valve is located at the exit of the right ventricle to the pulmonary arteries. The walls of the atria and ventricles consist of three layers: the epicardium, the myocardium, and the endocardium. The epicardium consists mostly of connective tissue and merges with the pericardial sac. The myocardium consists of muscle tissue, and the endocardium consists of a thin layer of epithelial tissue.

> **Review Video: The Heart**
> Visit mometrix.com/academy and enter code: 451399

Cardiac cycle

The cardiac cycle consists of diastole and systole phases, which can be further divided into the first and second phases to describe the events of the right and left sides of the heart. However, these events are simultaneously occurring. During the first diastole phase, blood flows through the superior and inferior venae cavae. Because the heart is relaxed, blood flows passively from the atrium through the open atrioventricular valve (tricuspid valve) to the right ventricle. The sinoatrial (SA) node, the cardiac pacemaker located in the wall of the right atrium, generates electrical signals, which are carried by the Purkinje fibers to the rest of the atrium, stimulating it to contract and fill the right ventricle with blood. The impulse from the SA node is transmitted to the ventricle through the atrioventricular (AV) node, signaling the right ventricle to contract and initiating the first systole phase. The tricuspid valve closes, and the pulmonary semilunar valve opens. Blood is pumped out the pulmonary arteries to the lungs. Blood returning from the lungs fills the left atrium as part of the second diastole phase. The SA node triggers the mitral valve to open, and blood fills the left ventricle. During the second systole phase, the mitral valve closes and the aortic semilunar valve opens. The left ventricle contracts and blood is pumped out of the aorta to the rest of the body.

Types of circulation

The circulatory system includes coronary circulation, pulmonary circulation, and systemic circulation. Coronary circulation is the flow of blood to the heart tissue. Blood enters the coronary arteries, which branch off the aorta, supplying major arteries, which enter the heart with oxygenated blood. The deoxygenated blood returns to the right atrium through the cardiac veins, which empty into the coronary sinus. Pulmonary circulation is the flow of blood between the heart and the lungs. Deoxygenated blood flows from the right ventricle to the lungs through pulmonary arteries. Oxygenated blood flows back to the left atrium through the pulmonary veins. Systemic circulation is the flow of blood to the entire body with the exception of coronary circulation and pulmonary circulation. Blood exits the left ventricle through the aorta, which branches into the carotid arteries, subclavian arteries, common iliac arteries, and the renal artery. Blood returns to the heart through the jugular veins, subclavian veins, common iliac veins, and renal veins, which

- 85 -

Copyright © Mometrix Media. You have been licensed one copy of this document for personal use only. Any other reproduction or redistribution is strictly prohibited. All rights reserved.

empty into the superior and inferior venae cavae. Included in systemic circulation is portal circulation, which is the flow of blood from the digestive system to the liver and then to the heart, and renal circulation, which is the flow of blood between the heart and the kidneys.

Review Video: Functions of the Circulatory System
Visit mometrix.com/academy and enter code: 376581

Roles in body's homeostasis

Circulatory system

The circulatory system is involved in numerous homeostatic relationships in the body. In general, the circulatory system regulates the levels of oxygen, nutrients, and wastes in the blood as required by cells to maintain life. The circulatory system assists the kidneys in maintaining the needed blood composition and blood volume while providing the needed pressure for the kidney's filtration system. The circulatory system works with the integumentary system, specifically the skin, to maintain a constant body temperature. If the body temperature is too high, blood capillaries near the surface of the skin dilate to release heat energy. If the body temperature is too low, blood capillaries near the surface of the skin restrict to keep warm blood from reaching the surface and preventing heat loss. The circulatory system also assists the endocrine system by delivering hormones.

Digestive system

The digestive system is involved in homeostatic relationships, including maintaining the pH balance and maintaining the balance of helpful bacteria. The pH varies throughout the digestive system. In the saliva, pH levels are only slightly acidic because saliva contains enzymes to digest starches and begin the digestive process. The teeth, mouth, throat, and esophagus are not harmed. In the stomach, the pH drops drastically because of the presence of hydrochloric acid (HCl), which destroys harmful pathogens. Because the stomach is lined with a mucous membrane, the stomach tissue is not harmed. With the aid of secretions from the pancreas, the pH is changed to the slightly basic range in the small intestine, which neutralizes the HCl in the chyme and aids in the function of enzymes needed to continue digestion. Helpful gut flora, consisting mostly of bacteria such as *Escherichia coli*, live in the digestive tract. Gut flora provides a variety of functions including the breaking down of polysaccharides, synthesizing vitamins B and K, and inhibiting the growth of harmful bacteria.

Process of digestion as food progresses through the alimentary canal

Digestion occurs in the alimentary canal (gastrointestinal tract), which consists of the mouth, throat (pharynx), esophagus, stomach, small intestine, large intestine, rectum, and anus. Digestion begins in the mouth as food is chewed and mixed with saliva containing enzymes for the digestion of carbohydrates (starches). Peristalsis, involuntary muscle contractions, moves the partially digested food down the esophagus and into the stomach through the lower esophageal sphincter. The stomach, which consists of three layers of smooth muscle lined with a mucous membrane, churns the food with hydrochloric acid (HCl). The stomach stores the chyme and releases it to the small intestine through the pyloric sphincter. The small intestine consists of three sections: the duodenum, jejunum, and ileum. The duodenum continues breaking down the food with help from the liver, gallbladder, and pancreas. The liver manufactures bile, which is stored in the gallbladder and secreted into the small intestine to aid in the digestion of fats. The pancreas secretes pancreatic juices, which aid in the digestion of carbohydrates, fats, and proteins. The pancreas secretes sodium bicarbonate to neutralize the HCl from the stomach. The jejunum and ileum contain numerous villi

Copyright © Mometrix Media. You have been licensed one copy of this document for personal use only. Any other reproduction or redistribution is strictly prohibited. All rights reserved.

for absorption. The large intestine, which houses helpful gut flora, consists of three sections called the ascending colon, transverse colon, and descending colon. The primary function of the large intestine is to absorb water. The rectum stores solid wastes (feces) until they exit the body through the anus.

Pituitary gland

The pituitary gland lies at the base of the brain just over the nasal cavity and is attached to the brain through the hypothalamus. The pituitary gland is considered to be the master gland of the endocrine system because it controls the other glands. The pituitary gland consists of the anterior and posterior lobes. The anterior lobe secretes five hormones including the human growth hormone (somatotropin) and the gonadotropins (prolactin or lactogenic hormone and follicle-stimulating hormone), which control hormones secreted by the reproductive organs. Additionally, the anterior lobe secretes thyroid-stimulating hormone (it regulates the thyroid gland) and adrenocorticotropic hormone (it regulates the adrenal gland). The posterior lobe of the pituitary gland releases two hormones that are actually produced by the hypothalamus: antidiuretic hormone (ADH) and oxytocin. The ADH, or vasopressin, works in conjunction with the kidneys to maintain the water balance in the body. Oxytocin stimulates uterine contractions during birth.

Location of pituitary gland and pineal gland

The pituitary gland and the pineal gland:

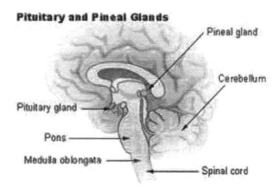

Pineal gland

The pineal gland lies between the cerebral hemispheres deep in the brain near the thalamus. The pineal gland secretes the hormone melatonin, which regulates the body's sleep cycle.

Thyroid gland and parathyroid glands

The thyroid and parathyroid glands are located in the neck just below the larynx. The parathyroid glands are four small glands that are embedded on the posterior side of the thyroid gland. The basic function of the thyroid gland is to regulate metabolism. The thyroid gland secretes the hormones thyroxine, triiodothyronine, and calcitonin. Thyroxine and triiodothyronine increase metabolism, and calcitonin decreases blood calcium by storing calcium in bone tissue. The hypothalamus directs the pituitary gland to secrete thyroid-stimulating hormone (TSH), which stimulates the thyroid gland to release these hormones as needed via a negative-feedback mechanism. The parathyroid glands secrete parathyroid hormone, which can increase blood calcium by moving calcium from the bone to the blood.

Copyright © Mometrix Media. You have been licensed one copy of this document for personal use only. Any other reproduction or redistribution is strictly prohibited. All rights reserved.

Role of pancreas in maintaining homeostasis of blood sugar

The pancreas plays a vital role in the homeostasis of blood sugar through clumps of endocrine glands referred to as the islets of Langerhans. The pancreas monitors blood sugar levels, and the islets of Langerhans secrete two hormones: glucagon and insulin. Glucagon signals the liver to convert glycogen to glucose and release it into the blood, and it stimulates the breakdown of fats into glucose. Insulin signals the body cells to remove glucose from the blood and stimulates the liver to store glucose as glycogen. This is accomplished through a negative-feedback loop. After a person eats, blood glucose levels rise and the beta cells are triggered to release of insulin, which signals the body to remove glucose from the blood. When blood glucose levels fall, the alpha cells release glucagon, which signals the liver to release glucose into the blood.

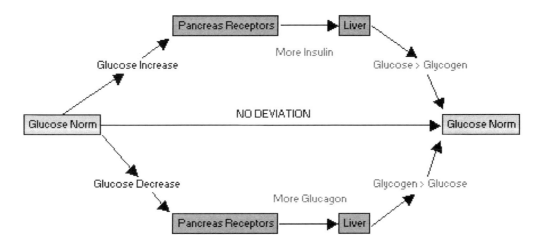

Adrenal glands

The adrenal glands are located on top of each kidney. The outer adrenal gland consists of two separate sections: the adrenal medulla (the inner portion) and the adrenal cortex (the outer portion). The hormones secreted by the adrenal cortex are essential for life, but the hormones secreted by the adrenal medulla are not essential for life. The adrenal medulla is controlled by the sympathetic nervous system and acts in times of distress or emergency by secreting epinephrine (adrenaline) and norepinephrine. The adrenal cortex, which is controlled by the hypothalamus through the pituitary gland, secretes two groups of hormones: mineralocorticoids and glucocorticoids. Aldosterone, a mineralocorticoid, works in the kidneys to regulate calcium and potassium concentrations and water balance in the blood. Cortisol (hydrocortisone), a glucocorticoid, helps regulate blood glucose levels, stimulates body repair, and acts as an inflammatory. The innermost adrenal cortex also secretes small amounts of androgens, or sex hormones, which contribute to the male sex characteristics.

Excretory system

Several organs help the body eliminate wastes and therefore can be considered part of the excretory system. The urinary system consists of the kidneys, ureters, urinary bladder, and urethra. The urinary system filters the blood of substances including urea, uric acid, ammonia, sodium chloride, and excess water. Although the sweat glands (integumentary system) function primarily in cooling the body, they also remove metabolic wastes including urea and salts. The colon (digestive system) removes excess bile and wastes from food products. The liver (digestive system)

- 88 -

Copyright © Mometrix Media. You have been licensed one copy of this document for personal use only. Any other reproduction or redistribution is strictly prohibited. All rights reserved.

removes poisons and toxins from the blood and pigments from dismantled red blood cells. The lungs (respiratory system) remove carbon dioxide wastes from the body.

Location and parts of the kidneys

The kidneys are bean-shaped structures that are located at the back of the abdominal cavity just under the diaphragm. Each kidney consists of three layers: the renal cortex (outer layer), renal medulla (inner layer), and renal pelvis (innermost portion). The renal cortex is composed of approximately one million nephrons, which are the tiny, individual filters of the kidneys. Each nephron contains a cluster of capillaries called a glomerulus surrounded by the cup-shaped Bowman's capsule, which leads to a tubule.

How kidneys filter blood

In general, the kidneys filter the blood, reabsorb needed materials, and secrete wastes and excess water in the urine. More specifically, blood flows from the renal arteries into arterioles into the glomerulus, where it is filtered. The glomerular filtrate enters the proximal convoluted tubule where water, glucose, ions, and other organic molecules are reabsorbed back into the bloodstream. Additional substances such as urea and drugs are removed from the blood in the distal convoluted tubule. Also, the pH of the blood can be adjusted in the distal convoluted tubule by the secretion of hydrogen ions. Finally, the unabsorbed materials flow out from the collecting tubules located in the renal medulla to the renal pelvis as urine. Urine is drained from the kidneys through the ureters to the urinary bladder, where it is stored until expulsion from the body through the urethra.

Role of kidneys in body's homeostasis of blood volume and blood pressure

In addition to their primary function of filtering the blood and removing wastes, the kidneys play several roles in the body's homeostasis including the regulation of blood volume and blood pressure. Hormones control the kidneys' regulation of the volume of the blood. Antidiuretic hormone (ADH), which is secreted by the posterior pituitary gland, increases the permeability of the distal tubule. If the blood volume drops too low, ADH is released, increasing the resorption of water. If the blood volume is too high, ADH is not released, and water is expelled in the urine. The blood volume affects blood pressure. As the blood volume increases, blood pressure increases. As the blood volume lowers, blood pressure lowers. Along with ADH, the renin-angiotensin-aldosterone system plays a critical role in controlling the kidneys. If the blood volume or blood pressure drops too low, renin is released by the kidneys. Renin is carried to the liver to aid in the formation of angiotensin I. Angiotensin I is carried to the lungs, where it is converted to angiotensin II. Angiotensin II is carried to the adrenal glands on top of the kidneys to trigger the release of aldosterone. Aldosterone signals the kidneys to conserve sodium and water, which increases blood volume and therefore blood pressure. When the blood volume and blood pressure increase, the hormone atrial natriuretic peptide (ANP) is released, which signals the halting of the renin-angiotensin-aldosterone system and helps to stabilize blood volume and blood pressure.

Immune system

The immune system protects the body against invading pathogens including bacteria, viruses, fungi, and protists. The immune system includes the lymphatic system (lymph, lymph capillaries, lymph vessel, and lymph nodes) as well as the red bone marrow and numerous leukocytes, or white blood cells. Tissue fluid enters the lymph capillaries, which combine to form lymph vessels. Skeletal muscle contractions move the lymph one way through the lymphatic system to lymphatic ducts, which dump back into the venous blood supply into the lymph nodes, which are situated along the lymph vessels, and filter the lymph of pathogens and other matter. The lymph nodes are concentrated in the neck, armpits, and groin areas. Outside the lymphatic vessel system lies the

- 89 -

Copyright © Mometrix Media. You have been licensed one copy of this document for personal use only. Any other reproduction or redistribution is strictly prohibited. All rights reserved.

lymphatic tissue including the tonsils, adenoids, thymus, spleen, and Peyer's patches. The tonsils, located in the pharynx, protect against pathogens entering the body through the mouth and throat. The thymus serves as a maturation chamber for the immature T cells that are formed in the bone marrow. The spleen cleans the blood of dead cells and pathogens. Peyer's patches, which are located in the small intestine, protect the digestive system from pathogens.

Leukocytes

Leukocytes, or white blood cells, are produced in the red bone marrow. Leukocytes can be classified as monocytes (macrophages and dendritic cells), granulocytes (neutrophils, basophils, and eosinophils), T lymphocytes, B lymphocytes, or natural killer cells. Macrophages engulf and destroy pathogens. Dendritic cells present antigens (foreign particles) to T cells. Neutrophils are short-living phagocytes that respond quickly to invaders. Basophils alert the body of invasion. Eosinophils are large, long-living phagocytes that defend against multicellular invaders. T lymphocytes or T cells include helper T cells, killer T cells, suppressor T cells, and memory T cells. Helper T cells help the body fight infections by producing antibodies and other chemicals. Killer T cells destroy cells that are infected with a virus or pathogen and tumor cells. Suppressor T cells stop or "suppress" the other T cells when the battle is over. Memory T cells remain in the blood on alert in case the invader attacks again. B lymphocytes, or B cells, produce antibodies.

Antigens

Antigens are substances that stimulate the immune system. Antigens are typically proteins on the surfaces of bacteria, viruses, and fungi. Substances such as drugs, toxins, and foreign particles can also be antigens. The human body recognizes the antigens of its own cells, but it will attack cells or substances with unfamiliar antigens. Specific antibodies are produced for each antigen that enters the body. In a typical immune response, when a pathogen or foreign substance enters the body, it is engulfed by a macrophage, which presents fragments of the antigen on its surface. A helper T cell joins the macrophage, and the killer (cytotoxic) T cells and B cells are activated. Killer T cells search out and destroy cells presenting the same antigens. B cells differentiate into plasma cells and memory cells. Plasma cells produce antibodies specific to that pathogen or foreign substance. Antibodies bind to antigens on the surface of pathogens and mark them for destruction by other phagocytes. Memory cells remain in the blood stream to protect against future infections from the same pathogen.

Integumentary system

The integumentary system, which consists of the skin including the sebaceous glands, sweat glands, hair, and nails, serves a variety of functions associated with protection, secretion, and communication. In the functions associated with protection, the integumentary system protects the body from pathogens and prevents various chemicals from entering the body. In the functions associated with secretion, sebaceous glands secrete sebum (oil) that waterproofs the skin, and sweat glands are associated with the body's homeostatic relationship of thermoregulation. Sweat glands also serve as excretory organs and help rid the body of metabolic wastes. In the functions associated with communication, sensory receptors distributed throughout the skin send information to the brain regarding pain, touch, pressure, and temperature. In addition to protection, secretion, and communication, the skin manufactures vitamin D and can absorb certain chemicals such as specific medications.

Copyright © Mometrix Media. You have been licensed one copy of this document for personal use only. Any other reproduction or redistribution is strictly prohibited. All rights reserved.

Layers of the skin and the subcutaneous layer

The layers of the skin from the surface of the skin inward are the epidermis and dermis. The subcutaneous layer lying below the dermis is also part of the integumentary system. The epidermis is the most superficial layer of the skin. The epidermis, which consists entirely of epithelial cells, does not contain any blood vessels. The deepest portion of the epidermis is the stratum basale, which is a single layer of cells that continually undergo division. As more and more cells are produced, older cells are pushed toward the surface. Most epidermal cells are keratinized. Keratin is a waxy protein that helps to waterproof the skin. As the cells die, they are sloughed off. The dermis lies directly beneath the epidermis. The dermis consists mostly of connective tissue. The dermis contains blood vessels, sensory receptors, hair follicles, sebaceous glands, and sweat glands. The dermis also contains elastin and collagen fibers. The subcutaneous layer or hypodermis is actually not a layer of the skin. The subcutaneous layer consists of connective tissue, which binds the skin to the underlying muscles. Fat deposits in the subcutaneous layer help to cushion and insulate the body.

Involvement of skin in temperature homeostasis

The skin is involved in temperature homeostasis or thermoregulation through the activation of the sweat glands. By thermoregulation, the body maintains a stable body temperature as one component of a stable internal environment. The temperature of the body is controlled by a negative feedback system consisting of a receptor, control center, and effector. The receptors are sensory cells located in the dermis of the skin. The control center is the hypothalamus, which is located in the brain. The effectors include the sweat glands, blood vessels, and muscles (shivering). The evaporation of sweat across the surface of the skin cools the body to maintain its tolerance range. Vasodilation of the blood vessels near the surface of the skin also releases heat into the environment to lower body temperature. Shivering is associated with the muscular system.

Sebaceous glands and sweat glands

Sebaceous glands and sweat glands are exocrine glands found in the skin. Exocrine glands secrete substances into ducts. In this case, the secretions are through the ducts to the surface of the skin. Sebaceous glands are holocrine glands, which secrete sebum. Sebum is an oily mixture of lipids and proteins. Sebaceous glands are connected to hair follicles and secrete sebum through the hair pore. Sebum inhibits water loss from the skin and protects against bacterial and fungal infections. Sweat glands are either eccrine glands or apocrine glands. Eccrine glands are not connected to hair follicles. They are activated by elevated body temperature. Eccrine glands are located throughout the body and can be found on the forehead, neck, and back. Eccrine glands secrete a salty solution of electrolytes and water containing sodium chloride, potassium, bicarbonate, glucose, and antimicrobial peptides. Eccrine glands are activated as part of the body's thermoregulation. Apocrine glands secrete an oily solution containing fatty acids, triglycerides, and proteins. Apocrine glands are located in the armpits, groin, palms, and soles of the feet. Apocrine glands secrete this oily sweat when a person experiences stress or anxiety. Bacteria feed on apocrine sweat and expel aromatic fatty acids, producing body odor.

Copyright © Mometrix Media. You have been licensed one copy of this document for personal use only. Any other reproduction or redistribution is strictly prohibited. All rights reserved.

Sebaceous glands and sweat glands:

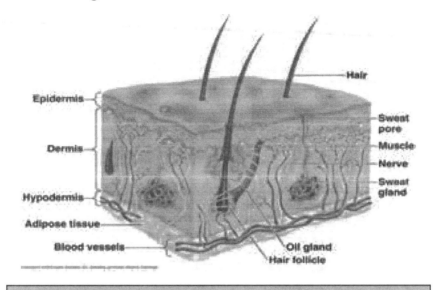

Review Video: <u>Functions of the Integumentary System</u>
Visit mometrix.com/academy and enter code: 398674

Muscular tissue

The three types of muscular tissue are skeletal muscle, smooth muscle, and cardiac muscle. Skeletal muscles are voluntary muscles that work in pairs to move various parts of the skeleton. Skeletal muscles are composed of muscle fibers (cells) that are bound together in parallel bundles. Skeletal muscles are also known as striated muscle due to their striped appearance under a microscope. Smooth muscle tissues are involuntary muscles that are found in the walls of internal organs such as the stomach, intestines, and blood vessels. Smooth muscle tissues or visceral tissue is nonstriated. Smooth muscle cells are shorter and wider than skeletal muscle fibers. Smooth muscle tissue is also found in sphincters or valves that control various openings throughout the body. Cardiac muscle tissue is involuntary muscle that is found only in the heart. Like skeletal muscle cells, cardiac muscle cells are also striated.

Major muscles

The human body has more than 650 skeletal muscles than account for approximately half of a person's weight. Starting with the head and face, the temporalis and masseter move the mandible (lower jaw bone). The orbicularis oculi closes the eye. The orbicularis oris draws the lips together. The sternocleidomastoids move the head. The trapezius moves the shoulder, and the pectoralis major, deltoid, and latissimus dorsi move the upper arm. The biceps brachii and the triceps brachii move the lower arm. The rectus abdominis, external oblique, and erector spine move the trunk. The external and internal obliques elevate and depress the ribs. The gluteus maximus moves the upper leg. The quadriceps femoris, hamstrings, and sartorius move the lower leg. The gastrocnemius and the soleus extend the foot.

Skeletal muscle contraction

Skeletal muscles consist of numerous muscle fibers. Each muscle fiber contains a bundle of myofibrils, which are composed of multiple repeating contractile units called sarcomeres. Myofibrils contain two protein microfilaments: a thick filament and a thin filament. The thick

- 92 -

Copyright © Mometrix Media. You have been licensed one copy of this document for personal use only. Any other reproduction or redistribution is strictly prohibited. All rights reserved.

filament is composed of the protein myosin. The thin filament is composed of the protein actin. The dark bands (striations) in skeletal muscles are formed when thick and thin filaments overlap. Light bands occur where the thin filament is overlapped. Skeletal muscle attraction occurs when the thin filaments slide over the thick filaments shortening the sarcomere. When an action potential (electrical signal) reaches a muscle fiber, calcium ions are released. According to the sliding filament model of muscle contraction, these calcium ions bind to the myosin and actin, which assists in the binding of the myosin heads of the thick filaments to the actin molecules of the thin filaments. Adenosine triphosphate released from glucose provides the energy necessary for the contraction.

Thermoregulation

Thermoregulation or temperature regulation is a homeostatic relationship involving the muscular system. Skeletal muscles and smooth muscles are involved in thermoregulation. If the body temperature drops below acceptable levels, the hypothalamus signals the body's warming mechanisms. Smooth muscles in the walls of blood vessels in the skin cause the blood vessels to constrict and divert blood into deeper tissues. Skeletal muscles are triggered, and shivering generates heat. When the body temperature rises back to acceptable levels, the hypothalamus signals the body's warming mechanisms to stop. Similarly, if the body temperature rises above acceptable levels, the blood vessels in the skin dilate by means of their smooth muscle tissue. As blood fills the skin's capillaries, heat is radiated away from the body.

Nervous system divisions

The nervous system consists of two major divisions: the central nervous system (CNS) and the peripheral nervous system (PNS). The CNS includes the brain and spinal cord. The brain is the major organ of the nervous system. The brain, which is divided into the cerebrum, cerebellum, and brain stem, controls the entire body including thinking, coordination of skeletal muscle movement, and involuntary actions such as breathing and heart rate. The brain communicates with the rest of the body via the spinal cord. The PNS includes the nerves that branch from the brain and spinal cord. As part of the PNS, 12 pairs of cranial nerves branch off the brain stem. Also extending from the spinal cord are 31 pairs of branching spinal nerves. The PNS includes the somatic nervous system and the autonomic nervous system. The somatic nervous system controls the five senses and the movement of skeletal muscles. The autonomic nervous system includes the sympathetic and parasympathetic nervous system. The sympathetic nervous system deals with stressful or emergency situations, and the parasympathetic nervous system returns the body to normal after stressful or emergency situations and maintains normal functioning.

Reflex arc

A reflex, the simplest act of the nervous system, is an automatic response without any conscious thought to a stimulus via the reflex arc. The reflex arc is the simplest nerve pathway, which bypasses the brain and is controlled by the spinal cord. For example, in the classic knee-jerk response (patellar tendon reflex), the stimulus is the reflex hammer hitting the tendon, and the response is the muscle contracting, which jerks the foot upward. The stimulus is detected by sensory receptors, and a message is sent along a sensory (afferent) neuron to one or more

Copyright © Mometrix Media. You have been licensed one copy of this document for personal use only. Any other reproduction or redistribution is strictly prohibited. All rights reserved.

interneurons in the spinal cord. The interneuron(s) transmit this message to a motor (efferent) neuron, which carries the message to the correct effector (muscle).

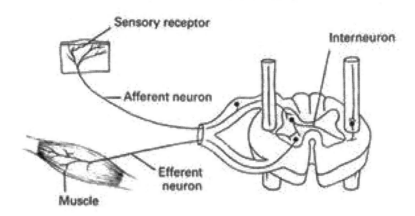

Autonomic nervous system

The autonomic nervous system (ANS) maintains homeostasis within the body. In general, the ANS controls the functions of the internal organs, blood vessels, smooth muscle tissues, and glands. This is accomplished through the direction of the hypothalamus, which is located above the midbrain. The hypothalamus controls the ANS through the brain stem. With this direction from the hypothalamus, the ANS helps maintain a stable body environment (homeostasis) by regulating numerous factors including heart rate, breathing rate, body temperature, and blood pH. The ANS consists of two divisions: the sympathetic nervous system and the parasympathetic nervous system. The sympathetic nervous system controls the body's reaction to extreme, stressful, and emergency situations. For example, the sympathetic nervous system increases the heart rate, signals the adrenal glands to secrete adrenaline, triggers the dilation of the pupils, and slows digestion. The parasympathetic nervous system counteracts the effects of the sympathetic nervous system. For example, the parasympathetic nervous system decreases heart rate, signals the adrenal glands to stop secreting adrenaline, constricts the pupils, and returns the digestion process to normal.

> **Review Video: Autonomic Nervous System**
> Visit mometrix.com/academy and enter code: 598501

Neurons

Types and functions

The three types of neurons are the sensory neurons, motor neurons, and interneurons. Sensory neurons transmit signals to the central nervous system (CNS) from the sensory receptors associated with touch, pain, temperature, hearing, sight, smell, and taste. Motor neurons transmit signals from the CNS to the rest of the body such as by signaling muscles or glands to respond. Interneurons transmit signals between neurons; for example, interneurons receive transmitted signals between sensory neurons and motor neurons.

Structure

In general, a neuron consists of three basic parts: the cell body, the axon, and many dendrites. The dendrites receive impulses from sensory receptors or interneurons and transmit them toward the

Copyright © Mometrix Media. You have been licensed one copy of this document for personal use only. Any other reproduction or redistribution is strictly prohibited. All rights reserved.

cell body. The cell body (soma) contains the nucleus of the neuron. The axon transmits the impulses away from the cell body. The axon is insulated by oligodendrocytes and the myelin sheath with gaps known as the nodes of Ranvier. The axon terminates at the synapse.

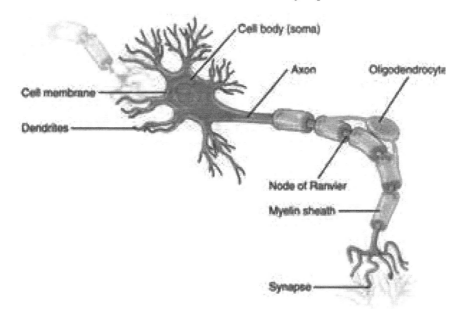

Male reproductive system

The male reproductive system produces, maintains, and transfers sperm and semen into the female reproductive tract and produces and secretes male hormones. The external structure includes the penis, scrotum, and testes. The penis, which contains the urethra, can fill with blood and become erect, enabling the deposition of semen and sperm into the female reproductive tract during sexual intercourse. The scrotum is a sac of skin and smooth muscle that houses the testes and keeps the testes at the proper temperature for spermatogenesis. The testes, or testicles, are the male gonads, which produce sperm and testosterone. The internal structure includes the epididymis, vas deferens, ejaculatory ducts, urethra, seminal vesicles, prostate gland, and bulbourethral glands.

The epididymis stores the sperm as it matures. Mature sperm moves from the epididymis through the vas deferens to the ejaculatory duct. The seminal vesicles secrete alkaline fluids with proteins and mucus into the ejaculatory duct, also. The prostate gland secretes a milky white fluid with proteins and enzymes as part of the semen. The bulbourethral glands, or Cowper's glands, secrete a fluid into the urethra to neutralize the acidity in the urethra. Additionally, the hormones associated with the male reproductive system include: follicle-stimulating hormone, which stimulates spermatogenesis; luteinizing hormone, which stimulates testosterone production; and testosterone, which is responsible for the male sex characteristics.

Female reproductive system

The functions of the female reproductive system are to produce ova (oocytes, or egg cells), transfer the ova to the fallopian tubes for fertilization, receive the sperm from the male, and to provide a protective, nourishing environment for the developing embryo.

External structures

The external portion of the female reproductive system includes the labia majora, labia minora, Bartholin's glands, and clitoris. The labia majora and the labia minora enclose and protect the

- 95 -

Copyright © Mometrix Media. You have been licensed one copy of this document for personal use only. Any other reproduction or redistribution is strictly prohibited. All rights reserved.

vagina. The Bartholin's glands secrete a lubricating fluid. The clitoris contains erectile tissue and nerve endings for sensual pleasure.

Internal structures

The internal portion of the female reproductive system includes the ovaries, fallopian tubes, uterus, and vagina. The ovaries, which are the female gonads, produce the ova and secrete estrogen and progesterone. The fallopian tubes carry the mature egg toward the uterus. Fertilization typically occurs in the fallopian tubes. If fertilized, the egg travels to the uterus, where it implants in the uterine wall. The uterus protects and nourishes the developing embryo until birth. The vagina is a muscular tube that extends from the cervix of the uterus to the outside of the body. The vagina receives the semen and sperm during sexual intercourse and provides a birth canal when needed.

Respiratory system

Components

The respiratory system can be divided into the upper and lower respiratory system. The upper respiratory system includes the nose, nasal cavity, mouth, pharynx, and larynx. The lower respiratory system includes the trachea, lungs, and bronchial tree. Alternatively, the components of the respiratory system can be categorized as part of the airway, the lungs, or the respiratory muscles. The airway includes the nose, nasal cavity, mouth, pharynx, (throat), larynx (voice box), trachea (windpipe), bronchi, and bronchial network. The airway is lined with cilia that trap microbes and debris and sweep them back toward the mouth. The lungs are structures that house the bronchi and bronchial network, which extend into the lungs and terminate in millions of alveoli (air sacs). The walls of the alveoli are only one cell thick, allowing for the exchange of gases with the blood capillaries that surround them. The right lung has three lobes. The left lung only has two lobes, leaving room for the heart on the left side of the body. The lungs are surrounded by a pleural membrane, which reduces friction between surfaces when breathing. The respiratory muscles include the diaphragm and the intercostal muscles. The diaphragm is a dome-shaped muscle that separates the thoracic and abdominal cavities. The intercostal muscles are located between the ribs.

Functions

The main function of the respiratory system is to supply the body with oxygen and rid the body of carbon dioxide. This exchange of gases occurs in millions of tiny alveoli, which are surrounded by blood capillaries. The respiratory system also filters air. Air is warmed, moistened, and filtered as it passes through the nasal passages before it reaches the lungs. The respiratory system is responsible for speech. As air passes through the throat, it moves through the larynx (voice box), which vibrates and produces sound, before it enters the trachea (windpipe). The respiratory system is vital in cough production. Foreign particles entering the nasal passages or airways are expelled from the body by the respiratory system. The respiratory system functions in the sense of smell. Chemoreceptors that are located in the nasal cavity respond to airborne chemicals. The respiratory system also helps the body maintain acid-base homeostasis. Hyperventilation can increase blood pH during acidosis (low pH). Slowing breathing during alkalosis (high pH) helps to lower blood pH.

Role in acid-base homeostasis

The respiratory system helps the body maintain acid-base homeostasis. For homeostasis, blood pH levels must be maintained in a range of approximately 7.38 to 7.42. The body's blood pH is maintained by the bicarbonate buffering system.

$$H_2O + CO_2 \leftrightarrow H_2CO_3 \leftrightarrow H^+ + HCO_3^-$$

Copyright © Mometrix Media. You have been licensed one copy of this document for personal use only. Any other reproduction or redistribution is strictly prohibited. All rights reserved.

The respiratory system is associated with the $H_2O + CO_2 \leftrightarrow H_2CO_3$ component of this equilibrium. Carbon dioxide dissociates in the blood, forming carbonic acid (H_2CO_3). The amount of carbonic acid in the blood determines the pH of the blood. The rate of breathing can raise or lower blood pH by raising or lowering the amount of carbon dioxide in the blood. If the blood pH drops too low (acidosis), the body increases breathing possibly even hyperventilating, which releases CO_2 from the blood and shifts the equilibrium to the left. This in turn raises the pH of the blood. If the blood pH becomes too high (alkalosis), the breathing rate slows, and CO_2 builds up in the blood. This causes the equilibrium to shift to the right and lowers the pH of the blood. The brain (medulla oblongata) monitors the level of carbon dioxide in the blood and signals the body to increase or decrease the rate of breathing accordingly. The kidneys also play a role in acid-base homeostasis.

Breathing process

During the breathing process, the diaphragm and the intercostal muscles contract to expand the lungs. During inspiration or inhalation, the diaphragm contracts and moves down, increasing the size of the chest cavity. During expiration or exhalation, the intercostal muscles contract and the ribs expand, increasing the size of the chest cavity. As the volume of the chest cavity increases, the pressure inside the chest cavity decreases (Boyle's law). Because the outside air is under a greater amount of pressure than the air inside the lungs, air rushes into the lungs. When the diaphragm and intercostal muscles relax, the size of the chest cavity decreases, forcing air out of the lungs. The breathing process is controlled by the portion of the brain stem called the medulla oblongata. The medulla oblongata monitors the level of carbon dioxide in the blood and signals the breathing rate to increase when these levels are too high.

Skeletal system

The skeletal system serves many functions including providing structural support, providing movement, providing protection, producing blood cells, and storing substances such as fat and minerals. The axial skeleton transfers the weight from the upper body to the lower appendages. Bones provide attachment points for muscles. The cranium protects the brain. The vertebrae protect the spinal cord. The rib cage protects the heart and lungs. The pelvis protects the reproductive organs. Joints including hinge joints, ball-and-socket joints, pivot joints, ellipsoid joints, gliding joints, and saddle joints. The red marrow manufactures red and white blood cells. All bone marrow is red at birth, but adults have approximately one-half red bone marrow and one-half yellow bone marrow. Yellow bone marrow stores fat.

Structure of axial skeleton and appendicular skeleton

The human skeletal system, which consists of 206 bones along with numerous tendons, ligaments, and cartilage, is divided into the axial skeleton and the appendicular skeleton. The axial skeleton consists of 80 bones and includes the vertebral column, rib cage, sternum, skull, and hyoid bone. The vertebral column consists of 33 vertebrae classified as cervical vertebrae, thoracic vertebrae, lumbar vertebrae, and sacral vertebrae. The rib cage includes 12 paired ribs, 10 pairs of true ribs and 2 pairs of floating ribs, and the sternum, which consists of the manubrium, corpus sterni, and xiphoid process. The skull includes the cranium and facial bones. The ossicles are bones in the middle ear. The hyoid bone provides an attachment point for the tongue muscles. The axial skeleton protects vital organs including the brain, heart, and lungs. The appendicular skeleton consists of 126 bones including the pectoral girdle, pelvic girdle, and appendages. The pectoral girdle consists of the scapulae (shoulders) and clavicles (collarbones). The pelvic girdle consists of two pelvic (hip) bones, which attach to the sacrum. The upper appendages (arms) include the humerus, radius, ulna, carpals, metacarpals, and phalanges. The lower appendages (legs) include the femur, patella, fibula, tibia, tarsals, metatarsals, and phalanges.

- 97 -

Copyright © Mometrix Media. You have been licensed one copy of this document for personal use only. Any other reproduction or redistribution is strictly prohibited. All rights reserved.

The axial skeleton and the appendicular skeleton:

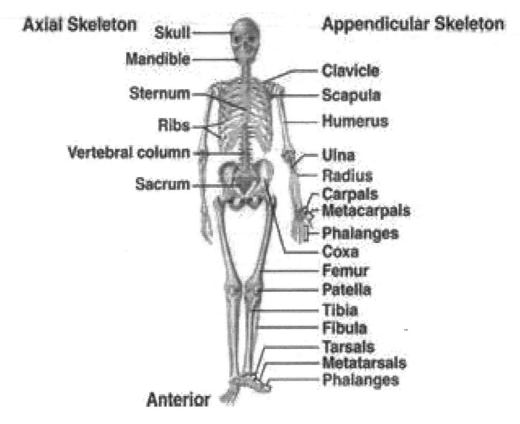

Compact and spongy bone

Two types of connective bone tissue include compact bone and spongy bone. Compact, or cortical, bone, which consists of tightly packed cells, is strong, dense, and rigid. Running vertically throughout compact bone are the Haversian canals, which are surrounded by concentric circles of bone tissue called lamellae. The spaces between the lamellae are called the lacunae. These lamellae and canals along with their associated arteries, veins, lymph vessels, and nerve endings are referred to collectively as the Haversian system. The Haversian system provides a reservoir for calcium and phosphorus for the blood. Also, bones have a thin outside layer of compact bone, which gives them their characteristic smooth, white appearance. Spongy, or cancellous, bone consists of trabeculae, which are a network of girders with open spaces filled with red bone marrow. Compared to compact bone, spongy bone is lightweight and porous, which helps reduce the bone's overall weight. The red marrow manufactures red and white blood cells. In long bones, the diaphysis consists of compact bone surrounding the marrow cavity and spongy bone containing red marrow in the epiphyses. Bones have varying amounts of compact bone and spongy bone depending on their classification.

Copyright © Mometrix Media. You have been licensed one copy of this document for personal use only. Any other reproduction or redistribution is strictly prohibited. All rights reserved.

Compact and spongy bone:

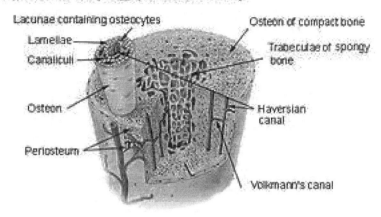

Compact Bone & Spongy (Cancellous Bone)

Lacunae containing osteocytes
Lamellae
Canaliculi
Osteon
Periosteum
Osteon of compact bone
Trabeculae of spongy bone
Haversian canal
Volkmann's canal

<u>Homeostatic relationship of remodeling</u>

Bone remodeling is a homeostatic relationship that is continually occurring throughout the skeletal system. In bone remodeling, bone is continually being removed and replaced with new bone. This job is performed by two special types of cells called osteoblasts and osteoclasts. Osteoclasts continually destroy mature bone tissue in a process called bone resorption, and osteoblasts continually construct new bone tissue including collagen fibers and hydroxyapatite crystals in a process called deposition. The osteoclasts secrete substances that dissolve the old matrix and carve out or construct the Haversian canals. The osteoblasts enter the Haversian canals and construct the needed collagen fibers and hydroxyapatite crystals. Weight-bearing exercise can increase the bone-building activity of the osteoblasts. Also, bone remodeling occurs when the body repairs a broken bone.

HIV and AIDS

The human immunodeficiency virus (HIV) impairs or destroys an infected individual's immune system, raising infection risk and ruining infection defenses. As HIV advances, its final stage is acquired immune deficiency syndrome (AIDS). The World Health Organization (WHO) estimated that by the end of 2013, 35 million humans were living with HIV. Of these, 23.4-26.2 million lived in sub-Saharan Africa. Anti-retroviral therapy (ART) drugs have enabled many HIV patients to survive 15+ years before developing AIDS symptoms. WHO estimated 12.9 million people were receiving these by the end of 2013, 11.7 million of them in low-income and middle-income nations.

Influenza

Influenza (flu) is an infectious viral respiratory illness. Its symptoms can range from mild to fatal. Young children, seniors, and people with some health conditions have greatest risk for serious complications. Annual vaccination is the best way to prevent it. Influenza pandemics—world outbreaks—occur when a new virus with little or no human immunity emerges. There were three in the 20th century and one so far in the 21st.

Cystic fibrosis

In cystic fibrosis (CF), a defective gene produces a protein causing the body to secrete mucus that is much thicker and stickier than normal. This mucus clogs up the lungs, resulting in infections that

Copyright © Mometrix Media. You have been licensed one copy of this document for personal use only. Any other reproduction or redistribution is strictly prohibited. All rights reserved.

can result in death. It also blocks the pancreas from delivering enzymes that help break down and absorb necessary nutrients from foods. Over 75 percent of CF patients are diagnosed by age 2. Today, almost half of CF patients are aged 18 or more. Around 1,000 new CF cases are diagnosed annually. Symptoms include shortness of breath; wheezing; chronic persistent coughing, including phlegm-productive coughs; slow weight gain and inadequate growth despite good appetite; frequently developing lung infections; difficult, bulky, greasy, and/or frequent bowel movements; and skin with an extremely salty taste. The life expectancy of individuals with CF has doubled in the past three decades.

Sickle cell anemia

Normal red blood cells are disc-shaped and travel easily through blood vessels. Sickle cell anemia is a condition in which the red blood cells are crescent-shaped, sticky, and stiff, impeding blood flow. This causes organ damage, pain, and increased risk of infections. Some patients have chronic fatigue and/or pain. Treatments enable some patients to live into their 40s, 50s, or older. In America, sickle cell anemia is most common in African-Americans (around one in 500).

Sickle cell anemia

Sickle cell anemia is a homozygous recessive genetic condition. When one parent has this gene but the other parent does not, children inherit sickle cell trait. The children do not have the disease, but may pass the sickle hemoglobin gene to their children. An individual who inherits a sickle cell gene from each parent (homozygote) will have sickle cell anemia. A heterozygote (one sickle cell gene) will not have sickle cell anemia and will advantageously be less susceptible to malaria.

Tay-Sachs disease

Tay-Sachs disease is a rare genetic disorder, inherited through an autosomal recessive pattern; i.e., both parents carry copies of a mutated gene and are usually asymptomatic, but pass these to their children. The genetic defect prevents an enzyme from breaking down a toxic substance, which builds up in the brain and spinal cord, progressively destroying neurons. The most common form appears in infancy. A typical sign is a "cherry-red spot" eye abnormality. Babies' motor muscles weaken. As the disease progresses, it causes seizures, loss of vision and hearing, intellectual impairment, and paralysis. Most children with the commoner infantile form of Tay-Sachs disease typically only survive until early childhood. Later-onset forms of the disease are extremely rare, typically with milder, highly variable symptoms including muscular weakness, poor coordination,

Copyright © Mometrix Media. You have been licensed one copy of this document for personal use only. Any other reproduction or redistribution is strictly prohibited. All rights reserved.

other motor symptoms, speech difficulties, and mental illness. Tay-Sachs is rare, but most common among European Jewish, Old-Order Pennsylvania Dutch/Amish, and Louisiana Cajun populations.

Diabetes

In type 1 diabetes, the pancreas fails to produce insulin; in type 2, the body becomes immune to insulin, causing chronically high, unstable blood sugar. Lifestyle factors such as obesity, poor nutrition, and physical inactivity can lead to type 2 diabetes. Blindness, limb loss, shock, coma, and death are possible results of uncontrolled diabetes. When people consume large amounts of refined carbohydrates (simple sugars and starches processed to remove all fibers) with no fiber slowing digestion, the sugars enter the bloodstream rapidly, causing a sudden spike in blood sugar, experienced by some as an energy rush. However, with quick metabolism and the pancreas' secretion of extra insulin to neutralize excessive blood sugar, sugars exit as fast as they entered, causing a precipitous blood-sugar drop, or "crash," with fatigue, sleepiness, irritability, depression and cycle-perpetuating cravings for more sugar or starch. During the development of type 2 diabetes the body becomes less sensitive to insulin, resulting in increased blood sugar levels.

Copyright © Mometrix Media. You have been licensed one copy of this document for personal use only. Any other reproduction or redistribution is strictly prohibited. All rights reserved.

Ecology

Biosphere

Components

The biosphere is the region of the earth inhabited by living things. The components of the biosphere from smallest to largest are organisms, populations, communities, ecosystems, and biomes. Organisms of the same species make up a population. All of the populations in an area make up the community. The community combined with the physical environment for a region forms an ecosystem. Several ecosystems are grouped together to form large geographic regions called biomes.

Population

A population is a group of all the individuals of one species in a specific area or region at a certain time. A species is a group of organisms that can breed and produce fertile offspring. There may be many populations of a specific species in a large geographic region. Ecologists study the size, density, and growth rate of populations to determine their stability. The population density is the number of individuals per unit of area. Growth rates may be exponential or logistic. Population size continuously changes with births, deaths, and migrations. Ecologists also study how the individuals are dispersed within a population. Some species form clusters. Others are evenly or randomly spaced. Every population has limiting factors. Changes in the environment can reduce population size. Geography can limit population size. The individuals of a population react with each other and with other organisms in the community. Competition and predation affect population size.

Community interactions

A community is all of the populations of different species that live in an area and interact with each other. Community interaction can be intraspecific or interspecific. Intraspecific interactions occur between members of the same species. Interspecific interactions occur between members of different species. Different types of interactions include competition, predation, and symbiosis. Communities with high diversity are more complex and more stable than communities with low diversity. The level of diversity can be seen in a food web of the community, which shows all the feeding relationships within the community.

Ecosystems

An ecosystem is the basic unit of ecology. An ecosystem is the sum of all the biotic and abiotic factors in an area. Biotic factors are all living things such as plants, animals, fungi, and microorganisms. Abiotic factors include the light, water, air, temperature, and soil in an area. Ecosystems obtain the energy they need from sunlight. Ecosystems contain biogeochemical cycles such as the hydrologic cycle and the nitrogen cycle. Ecosystems are generally classified as either terrestrial or aquatic. All of the living things within an ecosystem are called its community. The number and variety of living things within a community describes the ecosystem's biodiversity. Each ecosystem can only support a limited number of organisms known as the carrying capacity.

Biotic and abiotic factors in an ecosystem

Every ecosystem consists of multiple abiotic and biotic factors. Abiotic factors are the nonbiological physical and chemical factors that affect the ecosystem. Abiotic factors include soil type, atmospheric conditions, sunlight, water, wind, chemical elements, and natural disturbances. In aquatic ecosystems, abiotic factors include salinity, turbidity, water depth, current, temperature,

Copyright © Mometrix Media. You have been licensed one copy of this document for personal use only. Any other reproduction or redistribution is strictly prohibited. All rights reserved.

and light. Biotic factors are all of the living organisms in the ecosystem. Biotic factors include plants, algae, fungi, bacteria, archaea, animals, and protozoa.

Biomes

The biosphere consists of numerous biomes. A biome is a large region that supports a specific community. Each biome has a characteristic climate and geography. Differences in latitude, altitude, and worldwide patterns affect temperature, precipitation, and humidity. Biomes can be classified as terrestrial or aquatic biomes. Terrestrial biomes include ecosystems with land environments, such as tundra, coniferous forest, temperate broadleaf forest, temperate grassland, chaparral, desert, savannas, and tropical forests. Terrestrial biomes tend to grade into each other in regions called ecotones. Aquatic biomes are water-dwelling ecosystems. Aquatic biomes include lakes, coral reefs, rivers, oceanic pelagic zone, estuaries, intertidal zone, and the abyssal zone.

Aquatic biomes

Aquatic biomes are characterized by multiple factors including the temperature of the water, the amount of dissolved solids in the water, the availability of light, the depth of the water, and the material at the bottom of the biome. Aquatic biomes are classified as marine regions or freshwater biomes based on the amount of dissolved salt in the water. Marine biomes include the pelagic zone, the benthic zone, coral reefs, and estuaries. Marine biomes have a salinity of at least 35 parts per thousand. Freshwater biomes include lakes, ponds, rivers, and streams. Freshwater biomes have a salinity that is less than 0.5 parts per thousand. Lakes and ponds, which are relatively stationary, consist of two zones: the littoral zone and the limnetic zone. The littoral zone is closest to the shore and is home to many plants (floating and rooted), invertebrates, crustaceans, amphibians, and fish. The limnetic zone is further from the shore and has no rooted plants. Rivers and streams typically originate in the mountains and make their way to the oceans. Because this water is running and colder, it contains different plants and animals than lakes and ponds. Salmon, trout, crayfish, plants, and algae are found in rivers and streams.

Marine regions

Marine regions are located in three broad areas: the ocean, estuaries, and coral reefs. The ocean consists of two general regions—the pelagic zone and the benthic zone. The pelagic zone is in the open ocean. Organisms in the pelagic zone include phytoplankton such as algae and bacteria; zooplankton such as protozoa and crustaceans; and larger animals such as squid, sharks, and whales. The benthic zone consists of the floor and the ocean floor. Organisms in the benthic zone can include sponges, clams, oysters, starfish, sea anemones, sea urchins, worms, and fish. The deepest part of the benthic zone is called the abyssal plain. This is the deep ocean floor, which is home to numerous scavengers, many of which have light-generating capability. Estuaries are somewhat-enclosed coastal regions where water from rivers and streams is mixed with seawater. Coral reefs are located in warm, shallow water. Corals are small colonial animals that share a mutualistic relationship with algae.

Terrestrial biomes

Terrestrial biomes are classified predominantly by their vegetation, which is primarily determined by precipitation and temperature. Tropical rainforests experience the highest annual precipitation and relatively high temperatures. The dominant vegetation in tropical forests is tall evergreen trees. Temperate deciduous forests experience moderate precipitation and temperatures. The dominant vegetation is deciduous trees. Boreal forests experience moderate precipitation and lower temperatures. The dominant vegetation is coniferous trees. The tundra experiences lower

- 103 -

Copyright © Mometrix Media. You have been licensed one copy of this document for personal use only. Any other reproduction or redistribution is strictly prohibited. All rights reserved.

precipitation and cold temperatures. The dominant vegetation is shrubs. The savanna experiences lower precipitation and high temperatures. The dominant vegetation is grasses. Deserts experience the lowest precipitation and the hottest temperatures. The dominant vegetation is scattered thorny plants.

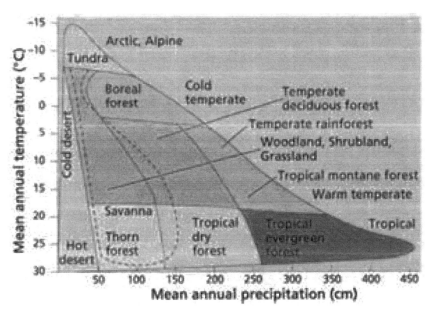

Influence of resource availability and abiotic factors on population size

Population size is affected by resource availability and abiotic factors. As the population density increases, intraspecific competition for available resources intensifies. If the availability of resources decreases, death rates may increase and birth rates may decrease. For example, territoriality for mating or nesting may limit available resources for individuals in a population and limit the population size. Abiotic factors such as temperature, rainfall, wind, and light intensity all influence the population size. For example, temperatures near a species' tolerance limit may decrease the population. Natural disasters such as fire or flood can destroy resources and greatly decrease a population's size. In general, any abiotic factor that reduces or limits resources will also reduce or limit population size.

Significance of habitat and niche to populations

The habitat of an organism is the type of place where an organism usually lives. A habitat is a piece of an environmental area. A habitat may be a geographic area or even the body of another organism. The habitat describes an organism's natural living environment. A habitat includes biotic and abiotic factors such as temperature, light, food resources, and predators. Whereas a habitat describes an organism's "home," a niche can be thought of as an organism's "occupation." A niche describes an organism's functional role in the community and how the organism uses its habitat. A niche can be quite complex because it should include the impacts that the organism has on the biotic and abiotic surroundings. Niches can be broad or narrow.

Influence of competition and predation on population size

Feeding relationships between organisms can affect population size. Competition and predation both tend to limit population size. Competition occurs when two individuals need the same resource. Predation occurs when one individual is the resource for another individual. Competition

- 104 -

Copyright © Mometrix Media. You have been licensed one copy of this document for personal use only. Any other reproduction or redistribution is strictly prohibited. All rights reserved.

occurs when individuals share a resource in the habitat. This competition can be intraspecific, which is between members of the same species, or interspecific, which is between members of different species. Intraspecific competition reduces resources as that species' own population increases. This limits population growth. Interspecific competition reduces resources as a different species uses those same resources. Predation occurs when one species is a food resource for another species. Predator and prey populations can cycle over a range of years. If prey resources increase, predator numbers increase. An example of the predator-prey population cycle is the Canadian lynx and snowshoe hare.

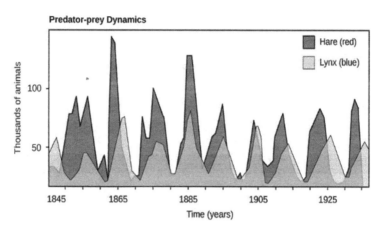

Logistic population growth model

Populations vary over time due to deaths, births, immigration, and emigration. In most situations, resources such as food, water, and shelter are limited. Each environment or habitat can only support a limited number of individuals. This is known as the carrying capacity. Population growth models that factor in the carrying capacity are called logistic growth models. With logistic population growth models, the rate of population growth decreases as the population size increases. Logistic growth graphs as an S-shaped curve. Comparing logistic growth and exponential growth shows that the graph for exponential growth continues to become steeper, but the graph for logistics growth levels off once the population reaches the carrying capacity. As the population increases, fewer resources are available per individual. This limits the number of individuals that can occupy that environment or habitat.

Exponential population growth model

Populations change over time due to births, deaths, and migrations. Sometimes, conditions are near ideal and populations can increase at their maximum rate exhibiting exponential growth. Exponential growth is growth in which the rate of change is proportional to the increasing size in an exponential progression. Exponential growth graphs as a J-shaped curve. Exponential growth is often observed in single-celled organisms such as bacteria or protozoa in which the population or number of cells increases by a factor of two per unit of time. One cell divides into two cells, which divide into four cells, and so forth. The exponential growth model describes population growth under ideal conditions. It does not take limiting factors or carrying capacity into account. Realistically, exponential growth cannot occur indefinitely, but it may occur for a period of time. It does show a species' capacity for increase and may be helpful when studying a particular species or ecosystem. For example, if a species with no natural predator is introduced into a new habitat, that species may experience exponential growth. If this growth is allowed to go unchecked, the population may overshoot the carrying capacity and then starve. Efforts may need to be taken to reduce the population before this occurs.

- 105 -

Copyright © Mometrix Media. You have been licensed one copy of this document for personal use only. Any other reproduction or redistribution is strictly prohibited. All rights reserved.

Advantages and disadvantages of asexual reproduction in animals

Very few species of animals reproduce by asexual reproduction, and nearly all of those species also have the ability to reproduce sexually. While not common, asexual reproduction is useful for animals that tend to stay in one place and may not find mates. Asexual reproduction takes considerably less effort and energy than sexual reproduction. In asexual reproduction, all of the offspring are genetically identical to the parent. This can be a disadvantage because of the lack of genetic variation. Although asexual reproduction is advantageous in a stable environment, if the environment changes, the organisms may lack the genetic variability to survive or selectively adapt.

Life histories

The life history of a species describes the typical organism's life cycle from birth through reproduction to death. Life histories can typically be classified as opportunistic life histories or equilibrial life histories. Species exhibiting opportunistic life histories are typically small, short-lived organisms that have a high reproductive capacity but invest little time and care into their offspring. Their population sizes tend to oscillate significantly over periods of several years. Species exhibiting equilibrial life histories are typically large, long-lived organisms that have a low reproductive capacity but invest much time and care into their offspring. Their populations tend to fluctuate within a smaller range. A general observation is that species that tend to produce numerous offspring typically tend to invest little care into that offspring, resulting in a high mortality rate of that offspring. Organisms of species that tend to produce few offspring typically invest much more care into that offspring, resulting in a lower mortality rate.

Symbiosis

Many species share a special nutritional relationship with another species, called symbiosis. The term symbiosis means "living together." In symbiosis, two organisms share a close physical relationship that can be helpful, harmful, or neutral for each organism. Three forms of symbiosis are parasitism, commensalism, and mutualism. Parasitism is a relationship between two organisms in which one organism is the parasite, and the other organism is the host. The parasite benefits from the relationship because the parasite obtains its nutrition from the host. The host is harmed from the relationship because the parasite is using the host's energy and giving nothing in return. For example, a tick and a dog share a parasitic relationship in which the tick is the parasite, and the dog is the host. Commensalism is a relationship between two organisms in which one benefits, and the other is not affected. For example, a small fish called a remora can attach to the belly of a shark and ride along. The remora is safe under the shark, and the shark is not affected. Mutualism is a relationship between two organisms in which both organisms benefit. For example, a rhinoceros usually can be seen with a few tick birds perched on its back. The tick birds are helped by the easy food source of ticks, and the rhino benefits from the tick removal.

Predation

Predation is a special nutritional relationship in which one organism is the predator, and the other organism is the prey. The predator benefits from the relationship, but the prey is harmed. The predator hunts and kills the prey for food. The predator is specially adapted to hunt its prey, and the prey is specially adapted to escape its predator. While predators harm (kill) their individual prey, predation usually helps the prey species. Predation keeps the population of the prey species under control and prevents them from overshooting the carrying capacity, which often leads to starvation. Also, predation usually helps to remove weak or slow members of the prey species

Copyright © Mometrix Media. You have been licensed one copy of this document for personal use only. Any other reproduction or redistribution is strictly prohibited. All rights reserved.

leaving the healthier, stronger, and better adapted individuals to reproduce. Examples of predator-prey relationships include lions and zebras, snakes and rats, and hawks and rabbits.

Competition and territoriality

Competition is a relationship between two organisms in which the organisms compete for the same vital resource that is in short supply. Typically, both organisms are harmed, but one is usually harmed more than the other. They could be competing for resources such as food, water, mates, and space. Interspecific competition is between members of different species. Intraspecific competition is between members of the same species. Competition provides an avenue for natural selection. Territoriality can be considered to be a type of interspecific competition for space. Many animals including mammals, birds, reptiles, fish, spiders, and insects have exhibited territorial behavior. Once territories are established, there are fewer conflicts between organisms. For example, a male redwing blackbird can establish a large territory. By singing and flashing his red patches, he is able to warn other males to avoid his territory, and they can avoid fighting.

Altruistic behaviors between animals

Altruism is a self-sacrificing behavior in which an individual animal may serve or protect another animal. For example, in a honey bee colony, there is one queen, many workers (females), and drones (males) only during the mating seasons. Adult workers do all the work of the hive and will die defending it. Another example of altruism is seen in a naked mole rat colony. Each colony has one queen that mates with a few males, and the rest of the colony is nonbreeding and lives to service the queen, her mates, and her offspring.

> **Review Video:** Mutualism, Commensalism, and Parasitism
> Visit mometrix.com/academy and enter code: 757249

Changes during primary and secondary succession

Ecological succession is the process by which climax communities come into existence or are replaced by new climax communities when they are greatly changed or destroyed. The two types of ecological succession are primary succession and secondary succession. Primary succession occurs in a region where there is no soil and that has never been populated such as a new volcanic island or a region where a glacier has retreated. During the pioneer stage, the progression of species is typically lichen and algae, followed by small annual plants, then perennial herbs and grasses. During the intermediate stage, shrubs, grasses, and shade-intolerant trees are dominant. Finally, after hundreds of years, a climax community is reached with shade-tolerant trees. Secondary succession occurs when a climax community is destroyed or nearly destroyed such as after a forest fire or in an abandoned field. With secondary succession, the area starts with soil and seeds from the original climax community. Typically, in the first two years, weeds and annuals are dominant. This is followed by grasses and biennials. In a few years, shrubs and perennials are dominant followed by pine trees, which are eventually replaced by deciduous trees. Secondary succession takes place in less than 100 years.

Energy flow through the environment

Energy pyramid

Energy flow through an ecosystem can be tracked through an energy pyramid. An energy pyramid shows how energy is transferred from one trophic level to another. Producers always form the base of an energy pyramid, and the consumers form successive levels above the producers. Producers

Copyright © Mometrix Media. You have been licensed one copy of this document for personal use only. Any other reproduction or redistribution is strictly prohibited. All rights reserved.

only store about 1% of the solar energy they receive. Then, each successive level only uses 10% of the energy of the previous level. In this energy pyramid, grass, which is a producer, uses 1,000 kcal of energy. Then the grasshoppers, which are primary consumers, use 10% of that 1,000 kcal or 100 kcal. Next, the moles, which are secondary consumers, use 10% of that 100 kcal or 10 kcal. Finally, the owl, which is a tertiary consumer, uses 10% of that 10 kcal or 1 kcal of energy.

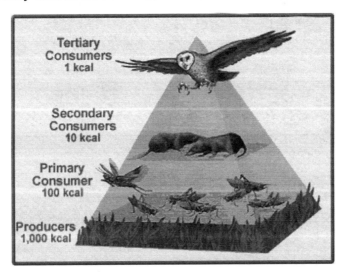

Food web

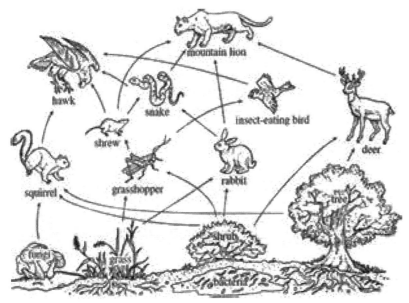

Energy flow through an ecosystem can be illustrated by a food web. Energy moves through the food web in the direction of the arrows. In the food web below, producers such as grass, trees, and shrubs use energy from the sun to produce food through photosynthesis. Herbivores or primary consumers such as squirrels, grasshoppers, and rabbits obtain energy by eating the producers. Secondary consumers, which are carnivores such as snakes and shrews, obtain energy by eating the primary consumers. Tertiary consumers, which are carnivores such as hawks and mountain lions, obtain energy by eating the secondary consumers. Note that the hawk and the mountain lion can

Copyright © Mometrix Media. You have been licensed one copy of this document for personal use only. Any other reproduction or redistribution is strictly prohibited. All rights reserved.

also be considered quaternary consumers in this food web if a different food chain within the web is followed.

Review Video: Food Webs
Visit mometrix.com/academy and enter code: 853254

Water cycle

The water cycle, also referred to as the hydrologic cycle, is a biogeochemical cycle that describes the continuous movement of the Earth's water. Water in the form of precipitation such as rain or snow moves from the atmosphere to the ground. The water is collected in oceans, lakes, rivers, and other bodies of water. Heat from the sun causes water to evaporate from oceans, lakes, rivers, and other bodies of water. As plants transpire, this water also undergoes evaporation. This water vapor collects in the sky and forms clouds. As the water vapor in the clouds cools, the water vapor condenses or sublimes depending on the conditions. Then, water moves back to the ground in the form of precipitation.

Copyright © Mometrix Media. You have been licensed one copy of this document for personal use only. Any other reproduction or redistribution is strictly prohibited. All rights reserved.

Carbon cycle

The carbon cycle is a biogeochemical cycle that describes the continuous movement of the Earth's carbon. Carbon is in the atmosphere, the soil, living organisms, fossil fuels, oceans, and freshwater systems. These areas are referred to as carbon reservoirs. Carbon flows between these reservoirs in an exchange called the carbon cycle. In the atmosphere, carbon is in the form of carbon dioxide. Carbon moves from the atmosphere to plants through the process of photosynthesis. Carbon moves from plants to animals through food chains. Carbon moves from living organisms to the soil when these organisms die. Carbon moves from living organisms to the atmosphere through cellular respiration. Carbon moves from fossil fuels to the atmosphere when fossil fuels are burned. Carbon moves from the atmosphere to the oceans and freshwater systems through absorption.

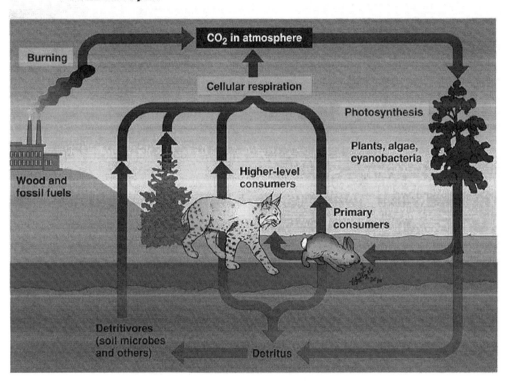

The carbon cycle

- 110 -

Copyright © Mometrix Media. You have been licensed one copy of this document for personal use only. Any other reproduction or redistribution is strictly prohibited. All rights reserved.

Nitrogen cycle

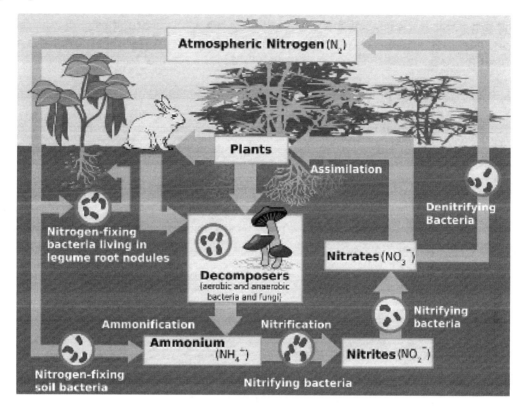

The nitrogen cycle is a biogeochemical cycle that describes the continuous movement of the Earth's nitrogen. Approximately 78% of the Earth's atmosphere consists of nitrogen in its elemental form N_2. Nitrogen is essential to the formation of proteins, but most organisms cannot use nitrogen in this form and require the nitrogen to be converted into some form of nitrates. Lightning can cause nitrates to form in the atmosphere, which can be carried to the soil by rain to be used by plants. Legumes have nitrogen-fixing bacteria in their roots, which can convert the N_2 to ammonia (NH_3). Nitrifying bacteria in the soil can also convert ammonia into nitrates. Plants absorb nitrates from the soil, and animals can consume the plants and other animals for protein. Denitrifying bacteria can convert unused nitrates back to nitrogen to be returned to the atmosphere.

- 111 -

Copyright © Mometrix Media. You have been licensed one copy of this document for personal use only. Any other reproduction or redistribution is strictly prohibited. All rights reserved.

Phosphorus cycle

The phosphorus cycle is a biogeochemical cycle that describes the continuous movement of the Earth's phosphorus. Phosphorus is found in rocks. When these rocks weather and erode, the phosphorus moves into the soil. The phosphorus found in the soil and rocks is in the form of phosphates or compounds with the PO_4^{3-} ion. When it rains, phosphates can be dissolved into the water. Plants are able to use phosphates from the soil. Plants need phosphorus for growth and development. Phosphorus is also a component of DNA, RNA, ATP, cell membranes, and bones. Plants and algae can absorb phosphate ions from the water and convert them into many organic compounds. Animals can get phosphorus by eating food or drinking water. When organisms die, the phosphorus is returned to the soil. This is the slowest of all biogeochemical cycles.

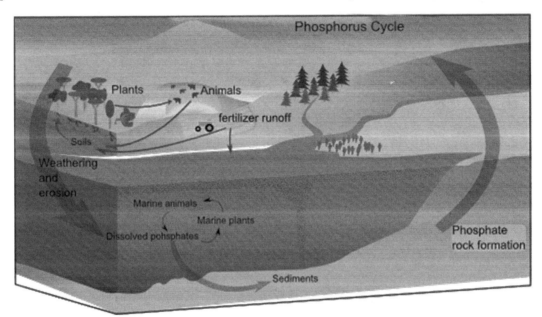

Natural disturbances that affect ecosystems

A natural disturbance is an event caused by nature, not human activity. Natural disturbances can be brought on by weather such as fires from lightning, droughts, storms, wind, and freezing. Other natural disturbances include earthquakes, volcanic eruptions, and diseases. Natural disturbances can disrupt or disturb the ecosystem in many ways such as altering resources or removing individuals from the community. Natural disturbances can cover small regions, or they can affect an entire ecosystem. The effect may be long lasting and take several years to recover, or the effect may be minor and take only a few months to recover.

Effect of fragmentation of ecosystems on biodiversity

Habitats can become fragmented due to natural disturbances such as fire, volcanic activity, and climate change. Some of the original habitat is destroyed during fragmentation, reducing the total area of the habitat. As a result, there may be insufficient food or other resources to support a species. The resulting habitats may also be reproductively isolated from each other, thus limiting genetic variation and biodiversity. Small fluctuations in resources or climate can be catastrophic in small populations. Larger populations may be able to overcome these fluctuations in variation.

Copyright © Mometrix Media. You have been licensed one copy of this document for personal use only. Any other reproduction or redistribution is strictly prohibited. All rights reserved.

Effects of human population on ecological systems and biodiversity

Human population has been increasing at a near-exponential rate for the past 50 years. As the human population increases, the demand for resources such as food, water, land, and energy also increases. As the human population increases, the number of species decreases due to habitat destruction, introduced species, and overhunting. The increased greenhouse gases and resulting climate changes have also significantly affected many ecosystems as temperatures rise and habitats are slowly changed or even destroyed. Increasing human population means increasing pollution, which harms habitats. Many animals have become extinct due to the effects of an exponentially increasing human population. High rates of extinction greatly reduce biodiversity.

Effects of habitat destruction by humans on ecological systems and biodiversity

Many habitats have been altered or destroyed by humans. In fact, habitat destruction brought about by human endeavors has been the most significant cause of species extinctions resulting in the decrease in biodiversity throughout the world. As the human population has increased exponentially, the extinction rate has also increased exponentially. This is largely due to habitat destruction by humans. Humans use many resources in their various enterprises including agriculture, industry, mining, logging, and recreation. Humans have cleared much land for agriculture and urban development. As habitats are destroyed, species are either destroyed or displaced. Often, habitats are fragmented into smaller areas, which only allow for small populations that are under threat by predators, diseases, weather, and limited resources. Especially hard hit are areas near the coastline, estuaries, and coral reefs. Nearly half of all mangrove ecosystems have been destroyed by human activity. Coral reefs have nearly been decimated from pollution such as oil spills and exploitation from the aquarium fish market and coral market.

Effects of introduced species on ecological systems and biodiversity

Introduced species are species that are moved into new geographic regions by humans. They are also called invasive or nonnative species. Introduction can be intentional, such as the introduction of livestock, or unintentional, such as the introduction of Dutch elm disease. Introduced species can disrupt their new communities by using limited resources and preying on other members of the community. Introduced species are often free from predators and can reproduce exponentially. This typically causes a decrease in biodiversity. Introduced species are contributors or even responsible for numerous extinctions. For example, zebra mussels, which are native to the Black Sea and the Caspian Sea, were accidentally introduced to the Great Lakes. The zebra mussels greatly reduced the amount of plankton available for the native mussel species, many of which are now endangered.

Impact of nonpoint sources of pollution on the environment

Nonpoint-source pollution is the leading cause of water pollution in the United States. Nonpoint-source pollution is pollution that does not flow through a pipe, channel, or container. Most nonpoint-source pollution is due to agricultural runoff. Urban runoff from lawns, streets, and parking lots is also treated as nonpoint-source pollution because much of that storm water does not go into a storm drain before entering streams, rivers, lakes, or other bodies of water. Urban runoff contains chemicals such as lawn fertilizers, motor oils, grease, pesticides, soaps, and detergents, each of which is harmful to the environment.

Copyright © Mometrix Media. You have been licensed one copy of this document for personal use only. Any other reproduction or redistribution is strictly prohibited. All rights reserved.

Effects of remediation on ecological systems and biodiversity

In remediation, or land rehabilitation, environmental damages is reversed or stopped by attempting to restore land to its prior condition. Examples of remediation are reforestation and mine reclamation. Mining reclamation includes the backfilling of open-pit mines and covering ores containing sulfides to prevent rain from mixing with them to produce sulfuric acid. Reforestation is the restocking of forests and wetlands. This can at least partially offset the damaging effects brought about by the deforestation. Reforestation can help reduce global warming due to an increase in the absorption of light by the trees. Restoration can also help to restore the carbon cycle and counter erosion. Reforestation can help maintain or preserve the biodiversity of the region and possibly increase biodiversity if new organisms immigrate into the region.

Pollution mitigation and the Clean Air Act

Pollution mitigation has greatly reduced pollution and its effects during the past 40 years. The Clean Air Act has reduced pollution by requiring that new industrial sites contain pollution-control technology. These technologies avoid or minimize the negative effects on the environment. For example, new coal-fired power plants are fitted with pollution-control devices that greatly reduce and nearly eliminate sulfur dioxide and nitrogen oxide emissions. This greatly reduces acid rain, improves water quality, and improves the overall health of ecosystems. Reducing acid rain improves soil quality, which in turn improves the health of producers, which consequently improves the health of consumers, essentially strengthening the entire ecosystem. Reduced greenhouse gas emissions have lessened the impact of global warming such as rising sea levels due to melting glaciers and the resulting loss of habitats and biodiversity. Reduced smog and haze improves the intensity of sunlight required for photosynthesis.

Resource management

Resource management such as waste management and recycling greatly impacts the environment. Waste management is the monitoring, collection, transportation, and recycling of waste products. Well-managed landfills include using clay or another lining material to prevent liquid leachate and layers of soil on top to reduce odors and vermin. Wastes can be incinerated to reduce waste volume. Hazardous biomedical waste can be incinerated. However, incineration does emit pollutants and greenhouse gases. Proper waste management always includes recycling. Recycling is a method to recover resources. Recycled materials can be reprocessed into new products. Metals such as aluminum, copper, and steel are recycled. Plastics, glass, and paper products can be recycled. Organic materials such as plant materials and food scraps can be composted. The current trend is to shift from waste management to resource recovery. Wastes should be minimized and reduced to minimize the need for disposal. Unavoidable nonrecyclable wastes should be converted to energy by combustion if at all possible.

Impact of global warming, rising sea levels, and flooding on society

Global warming caused largely by greenhouse gas emission will greatly affect society in the next several years. The increase in global temperature leads to more extreme weather events such as hurricanes, tornadoes, floods, and droughts. Rising temperatures mean warmer summers. Warmer temperatures may shift tourism and improve agriculture, but global mortality rates may rise due to hotter heat waves. Rising temperatures cause weather patterns to shift, leading to more floods and droughts. Rising temperatures mean a decrease in glaciers, sea ice, ice sheets, and snow cover, which all contribute to rising sea levels. Rising sea levels lead to habitat change or loss, which greatly affects numerous species. Some motile species are already moving north to cooler climates.

Copyright © Mometrix Media. You have been licensed one copy of this document for personal use only. Any other reproduction or redistribution is strictly prohibited. All rights reserved.

Earlier snowmelt and runoff may overwhelm water management systems. Diseases such as malaria that are spread by mosquitoes could spread further, possibly even to temperate regions. Rising sea levels mean higher storm surges and related issues.

Endangered Species Act

The Endangered Species Act (ESA) of 1973 has had a positive impact on many species. The law was designed to protect "imperiled species" from extinction due to factors such as loss of habitat, overhunting, and lack of conservation. The ESA also protects the species' ecosystems and removes threats to those ecosystems. If an animal is placed on the endangered or threatened list, it is prohibited to "harass, harm, pursue, hunt, shoot, wound, kill, trap, capture, or collect, or to attempt to engage in any such conduct" with the endangered animal. The populations of many species have increased significantly, including the whooping crane, the gray wolf, the red wolf, and the Hawaiian goose. Some species have even been removed from the endangered species list, including the bald eagle, the peregrine falcon, the gray whale, and the grizzly bear. The ESA has protected numerous species while balancing human economic needs and rights to private property.

National Park System

The purpose of the National Park System is to "conserve the scenery and the natural and historic objects and the wildlife therein and to provide for the enjoyment of the same in such manner and by such means as will leave them unimpaired for the enjoyment of future generations." The National Park System protects complete ecosystems and houses great biodiversity. National parks are an integral part of the survival of many species. National parks provide a home to hundreds of endangered or threatened species. Studies show that preserved habitats near national parks helps many species better survive. This will prevent fragmentation and further habitat loss. Nevertheless, National parks may be threatened by invasion species or pressure for use of land along park boundaries. Also, biodiversity is threatened even within national parks. Although many are vast, they still may not be large enough to support a species population.

Effects of extraction of minerals and oil drilling

The extraction of mineral and energy resources by mining and drilling has harmful effects on the environment including pollution and alterations to ecosystems. Mining requires large amounts of land, which harms habitats and affects biodiversity. Mining causes water pollution. Rainwater mixes with the heavy metals in mines and produces an acid runoff that harms aquatic life, birds, and mammals. The pollution is especially bad in countries without proper mining regulations. Open-pit mines and mountaintop removal techniques are especially harsh to the environment, and reclamation is often not regulated in developing countries. Mining often requires large-scale deforestation leading to a loss of habitat for many species. Toxic chemicals such as mercury and sulfuric acid are used in the mining process and are released into bodies of water, harming the aquatic life. If these toxic chemicals are leaked, the ground water is polluted. Oil drilling is controversial due to habitat disruption or loss. Oil spills are toxic to wildlife and difficult to clean up. Offshore drilling uses seismic waves to locate oil, which disturbs whales and dolphins and has been tied to hundreds of beached whales.

Sustainable agriculture

The management of natural resources and the renewability or sustainability of those natural resources greatly impact society. Sustainable agriculture involves growing foods in economical ways that do not harm resources. If left unchecked, farming can deplete the soil of valuable nutrients. Crops grown in these depleted soils are less healthy and more susceptible to disease.

- 115 -

Copyright © Mometrix Media. You have been licensed one copy of this document for personal use only. Any other reproduction or redistribution is strictly prohibited. All rights reserved.

Sustainable agriculture uses more effective pest control such as insect-resistant corn, which reduces runoff and water pollution in the surrounding area. Sustainable forestry involves replenishing trees as trees are being harvested, which maintains the environment.

Renewable and nonrenewable energy resources

Energy sources such as wind, solar power, and biomass energy are all renewable. Wind power is clean with no pollution and no greenhouse gas emissions. Disadvantages of wind power include the use of land for wind farms, threats to birds, and the expense to build. Solar power has no greenhouse gas emissions, but some toxic metal wastes result in the production of photovoltaic cells, and solar power requires large areas of land. Biomass energy is sustainable, but its combustion produces greenhouse emissions. Farming biomass requires large areas of land. Fossil fuels, which are nonrenewable, cause substantially more air pollution and greenhouse gas emissions, contributing to habitat loss and global warming.

Copyright © Mometrix Media. You have been licensed one copy of this document for personal use only. Any other reproduction or redistribution is strictly prohibited. All rights reserved.

NYSTCE Practice Test

Molecular and Cellular Biology

1. The hydrogen bonds in a water molecule make water a good
   a. Solvent for lipids
   b. Participant in replacement reactions
   c. Surface for small particles and living organisms to move across
   d. Solvent for polysaccharides such as cellulose
   e. Example of an acid

2. The breakdown of a disaccharide releases energy which is stored as ATP. This is an example of a(n)
   a. Combination reaction
   b. Replacement reaction
   c. Endothermic reaction
   d. Exothermic reaction
   e. Thermodynamic reaction

3. Which of the following metabolic compounds is composed of only carbon, oxygen, and hydrogen?
   a. Phospholipids
   b. Glycogen $C \quad O \quad H$
   c. Peptides
   d. RNA
   e. Vitamins

4. When an animal takes in more energy that it uses over an extended time, the extra chemical energy is stored as:
   a. Fat
   b. Starch
   c. Protein
   d. Enzymes
   e. Cholesterol

5. Which of the following molecules is thought to have acted as the first enzyme in early life on earth?
   a. Protein
   b. RNA
   c. DNA
   d. Triglycerides
   e. Phospholipids

6. Which of the following organelles is/are formed when the plasma membrane surrounds a particle outside of the cell?
   a. Golgi bodies
   b. Rough endoplasmic reticulum
   c. Lysosomes
   d. Secretory vesicles
   e. Endocytic vesicles

- 117 -

Copyright © Mometrix Media. You have been licensed one copy of this document for personal use only. Any other reproduction or redistribution is strictly prohibited. All rights reserved.

7. Which of the following plant organelles contain(s) pigment that give leaves their color?

    a. Centrioles
    b. Cell walls
    c. Chloroplasts
    d. Central vacuole
    e. Golgi apparatus

8. All but which of the following processes are ways of moving solutes across a plasma membrane?

    a. Osmosis
    b. Passive transport
    c. Active transport
    d. Facilitated diffusion
    e. Endocytosis

9. Prokaryotic and eukaryotic cells are similar in having which of the following?

    a. Membrane-bound organelles
    b. Protein-studded DNA
    c. Presence of a nucleus
    d. Integral membrane proteins in the plasma membrane
    e. Flagella composed of microtubules

10. Which of the following cell types has a peptidoglycan cell wall?

    a. Algae
    b. Bacteria
    c. Fungi
    d. Land plants
    e. Protists

11. Enzymes catalyze biochemical reactions by

    a. Lowering the potential energy of the products
    b. Separating inhibitors from products
    c. Forming a complex with the products
    d. Lowering the activation energy of the reaction
    e. Providing energy to the reaction

12. Which of the following is an example of a cofactor?

    a. Zinc
    b. Actin
    c. Cholesterol
    d. GTP
    e. Chlorophyll

13 Cyanide is a poison that binds to the active site of the enzyme cytochrome c and prevents its activity. Cyanide is a(n)

    a. Prosthetic group
    b. Cofactor
    c. Coenzyme
    d. Inhibitor
    e. Reverse regulator

Copyright © Mometrix Media. You have been licensed one copy of this document for personal use only. Any other reproduction or redistribution is strictly prohibited. All rights reserved.

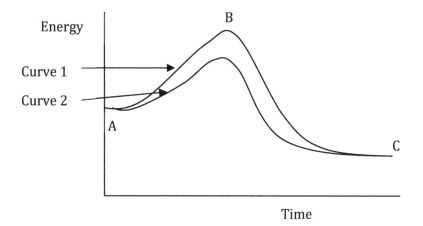

Time

14. The graph above shows the potential energy of molecules during the process of a chemical reaction. All of the following may be true EXCEPT

    a. This is an endergonic reaction
    b. The activation energy in curve 2 is less than the activation energy in curve 1
    c. The energy of the products is less than the energy of the substrate
    d. Curve 2 shows the reaction in the presence of an enzyme
    e. The reaction required ATP

15. Which of the following is not a characteristic of enzymes?

    a. They change shape when they bind their substrates
    b. They can catalyze reactions in both forward and reverse directions
    c. Their activity is sensitive to changes in temperature
    d. They are always active on more than one kind of substrate
    e. They may have more than one binding site

16. In a strenuously exercising muscle, NADH begins to accumulate in high concentration. Which of the following metabolic process will be activated to reduce the concentration of NADH?

    a. Glycolysis
    b. The Krebs cycle
    c. Lactic acid fermentation
    d. Oxidative phosphorylation
    e. Acetyl CoA synthesis

17. Which of the following statements regarding chemiosmosis in mitochondria is not correct?

    a. ATP synthase is powered by protons flowing through membrane channels
    b. Energy from ATP is used to transport protons to the intermembrane space
    c. Energy from the electron transport chain is used to transport protons to the intermembrane space
    d. An electrical gradient and a pH gradient both exist across the inner membrane
    e. The waste product of chemiosmosis is water

- 119 -

Copyright © Mometrix Media. You have been licensed one copy of this document for personal use only. Any other reproduction or redistribution is strictly prohibited. All rights reserved.

18. In photosynthesis, high-energy electrons move through electron transport chains to produce ATP and NADPH. Which of the following provides the energy to create high energy electrons?

    a. NADH
    b. NADP+
    c. O2
    d. Water
    e. Light

19. Which of the following kinds of plants is most likely to perform CAM photosynthesis?

    a. Mosses
    b. Grasses
    c. Deciduous trees
    d. Cacti
    e. Legumes

20. The combination of DNA with histones is called

    a. A centromere
    b. Chromatin
    c. A chromatid
    d. Nucleoli
    e. A plasmid

21. How many chromosomes does a human cell have after meiosis I?

    a. 92
    b. 46
    c. 23
    d. 22
    e. 12

22. In plants and animals, genetic variation is introduced during

    a. Crossing over in mitosis
    b. Chromosome segregation in mitosis
    c. Cytokinesis of meiosis
    d. Anaphase I of meiosis
    e. Anaphase II of meiosis

23. DNA replication occurs during which of the following phases?

    a. Prophase I
    b. Prophase II
    c. Interphase I
    d. Interphase II
    e. Telophase I

24. The synaptonemal complex is present in which of the following phases of the cell cycle?

    a. Metaphase of mitosis
    b. Prophase of meiosis I
    c. Telophase of meiosis I
    d. Metaphase of meiosis II
    e. Telophase of meiosis II

Copyright © Mometrix Media. You have been licensed one copy of this document for personal use only. Any other reproduction or redistribution is strictly prohibited. All rights reserved.

25. A length of DNA coding for a particular protein is called a(n)

a. Allele
b. Genome
c. Gene
d. Transcript
e. Codon

26. In DNA replication, which of the following enzymes is required for separating the DNA molecule into two strands?

a. DNA polymerase
b. Single strand binding protein
c. DNA gyrase
d. Helicase
e. Primase

27. Which of the following chemical moieties forms the backbone of DNA?

a. Nitrogenous bases
b. Glycerol
c. Amino groups
d. Pentose and phosphate
e. Glucose and phosphate

28. Which of the following is required for the activity of DNA polymerase?

a. Okazaki fragments
b. RNA primer
c. Single-strand binding protein
d. Leading strand
e. Replication fork

29. Which of the following is the substrate for DNA ligase?

a. Okazaki fragments
b. RNA primer
c. Single-strand binding protein
d. Leading strand
e. Replication fork

30. Which of the following is true of the enzyme telomerase?

a. It is active on the leading strand during DNA synthesis
b. It requires a chromosomal DNA template
c. It acts in the $3' \rightarrow 5'$ direction
d. It adds a repetitive DNA sequence to the end of chromosomes
e. It takes the place of primase at the ends of chromosomes

31. Which enzyme in DNA replication is a potential source of new mutations?

a. DNA ligase
b. Primase
c. DNA gyrase
d. DNA polymerase
e. Topoisomerase

Copyright © Mometrix Media. You have been licensed one copy of this document for personal use only. Any other reproduction or redistribution is strictly prohibited. All rights reserved.

32. Which of the following mutations is most likely to have a dramatic effect on the sequence of a protein?

    a. A point mutation
    b. A missense mutation
    c. A deletion
    d. A silent mutation
    e. A proofreading mutation

33. Which of the following could be an end product of transcription?

    a. rRNA
    b. DNA
    c. Protein
    d. snRNP
    e. Amino acids

34. The *lac* operon controls

    a. Conjugation between bacteria
    b. Chromatin organization
    c. Gene transcription
    d. Excision repair
    e. Termination of translation

35. All of the following are examples ways of controlling eukaryotic gene expression EXCEPT

    a. Regulatory proteins
    b. Nucleosome packing
    c. Methylation of DNA
    d. RNA interference
    e. Operons

36. Transfer of DNA between bacteria using a narrow tube called a pilus is called

    a. Transformation
    b. Transduction
    c. Operation
    d. Conjugation
    e. Conformation

37. A virus that has incorporated into the DNA of its host

    a. Lysogenic cycle
    b. Lytic cycle
    c. Retrovirus
    d. Provirus
    e. Bacteriophage

38. A virus in this stage is actively replicating DNA

    a. Lysogenic cycle
    b. Lytic cycle
    c. Retrovirus
    d. Provirus
    e. Bacteriophage

Copyright © Mometrix Media. You have been licensed one copy of this document for personal use only. Any other reproduction or redistribution is strictly prohibited. All rights reserved.

39. A bacterial mini-chromosome used in recombinant DNA technology is called a
    a. Centromere
    b. Telomere
    c. Plasmid
    d. Transposon
    e. cDNA

Copyright © Mometrix Media. You have been licensed one copy of this document for personal use only. Any other reproduction or redistribution is strictly prohibited. All rights reserved.

Organismal Biology

40. Which of the following parts of an angiosperm give rise to the fruit?

    a. Pedicel
    b. Filament
    c. Sepal
    d. Ovary
    e. Meristem

41. Which of the following structures is NOT present in gymnosperms?

    a. Leaves
    b. Pollen
    c. Flowers
    d. Stomata
    e. Roots

42. Which of the following plant structures allows for gas exchange?

    a. Xylem
    b. Phloem
    c. Cuticle
    d. Meristem
    e. Stomata

43. Which type of plant has leaves with parallel veins?

    a. Monocots
    b. Dicots
    c. Angiosperms
    d. Gymnosperms
    e. Nonvascular plants

44. Which type of plant does not produce fruits

    a. Monocots
    b. Dicots
    c. Angiosperms
    d. Gymnosperms
    e. Nonvascular plants

45. Which type of plant produces seeds that are housed inside a fruit

    a. Monocots
    b. Dicots
    c. Angiosperms
    d. Gymnosperms
    e. Nonvascular plants

Questions 46 and 47 pertain to the following diagram representing a cross section of a tree trunk

Copyright © Mometrix Media. You have been licensed one copy of this document for personal use only. Any other reproduction or redistribution is strictly prohibited. All rights reserved.

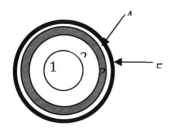

46. Which structure contains tissue that is dead at maturity?

    a. 1
    b. 2
    c. 3
    d. 4
    e. 5

47. Which structure transports carbohydrates to the roots?

    a. 1
    b. 2
    c. 3
    d. 4
    e. 5

48. In ferns, the joining of egg and sperm produces a zygote, which will grow into the

    a. Gametophyte
    b. Sporophyte
    c. Spore
    d. Sporangium
    e. Seedling

49. Which of the following is an example of the alternation of generations life cycle?

    a. Asexual reproduction of strawberries by runners
    b. Annual plants that live through a single growing season
    c. Ferns that have a large diploid and a diminutive haploid stage
    d. Insects that have distinct larval and adult stages
    e. Reptiles that have long periods of dormancy and metabolic inactivity

Questions 50 and 51 pertain to the following diagram of a complete, perfect flower

Copyright © Mometrix Media. You have been licensed one copy of this document for personal use only. Any other reproduction or redistribution is strictly prohibited. All rights reserved.

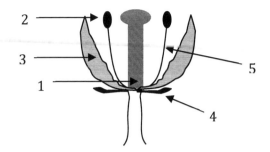

50. The structure in which microspores are produced.

    a. 1
    b. 2
    c. 3
    d. 4
    e. 5

51. The structures composed solely of diploid cells

    a. 1, 2, and 3
    b. 2, 3, and 4
    c. 3, 4, and 5
    d. 1, 4, and 5
    e. 1, 2, and 4

52. Auxins are plant hormones that are involved in all but which of the following processes?

    a. Fruit ripening
    b. Gravitropism
    c. Growth
    d. Phototropism
    e. Seed germination

53. Which of the following plant hormones is most likely to delay aging when sprayed on cut flowers and fruit?

    a. Ethylene
    b. Gibberellins
    c. Cytokinins
    d. Abscisic acid
    e. Jasmonic acid

54. Which of the following would most likely be disruptive to the flowering time of a day-neutral plant?

    a. Daylight interrupted by a brief dark period
    b. Daylight interrupted by a long dark period
    c. High daytime temperatures
    d. Night interrupted by a brief exposure to red light
    e. Night interrupted by a long exposure to red light

Copyright © Mometrix Media. You have been licensed one copy of this document for personal use only. Any other reproduction or redistribution is strictly prohibited. All rights reserved.

55. Animals exchange gases with the environment in all of the following ways EXCEPT
   a. Direct exchange through the skin
   b. Exchange through gills
   c. Stomata
   d. Tracheae
   e. Lungs

56. Which of the following blood components is involved in blood clotting?
   a. Red blood cells
   b. Platelets
   c. White blood cells
   d. Leukocytes
   e. Plasma

57. Which section of the digestive system is responsible for water reabsorption?
   a. The large intestine
   b. The duodenum
   c. The small intestine
   d. The gallbladder
   e. The stomach

58. When Ca^{2+} channels open in a presynaptic cell (doesn't the cell also depolarize?)
   a. The cell depolarizes
   b. The cell hyperpolarizes
   c. An action potential is propagated
   d. Synaptic vesicles release neurotransmitter
   e. The nerve signal is propagated by salutatory conduction

59. Which of the following processes is an example of positive feedback?
   a. High CO2 blood levels stimulate respiration which decreases blood CO2 levels
   b. High blood glucose levels stimulate insulin release, which makes muscle and liver cells take in glucose
   c. Increased nursing stimulates increased milk production in mammary glands
   d. Low blood oxygen levels stimulate erythropoietin production which increases red blood cell production by bone marrow
   e. Low blood calcium levels stimulate parathyroid hormone release from the parathyroid gland. Parathyroid hormone stimulates calcium release from bones.

60. Which of the following would be the most likely means of thermoregulation for a mammal in a cold environment?
   a. Adjusting body surface area
   b. Sweating
   c. Countercurrent exchange
   d. Muscle contractions
   e. Increased blood flow to extremities

Copyright © Mometrix Media. You have been licensed one copy of this document for personal use only. Any other reproduction or redistribution is strictly prohibited. All rights reserved.

61. Which hormone is *not* secreted by a gland in the brain?

  a. Human chorionic gonadotropin (HCG)
  b. Gonadotropin releasing hormone (GnRH)
  c. Luteinizing hormone (LH)
  d. Follicle stimulating hormone (FSH)
  e. None of these

62. Which hormone is secreted by the placenta throughout pregnancy?

  a. Human chorionic gonadotropin (HCG)
  b. Gonadotropin releasing hormone (GnRH)
  c. Luteinizing hormone (LH)
  d. Follicle stimulating hormone (FSH)
  e. None of these

63. Polar bodies are a by-product of

  a. Meiosis I
  b. Meiosis II
  c. Both meiosis I and II
  d. Zygote formation
  e. Mitosis of the morula

64. Which of the following hormones triggers ovulation in females?

  a. Estrogen
  b. Progesterone
  c. Serotonin
  d. Luteinizing hormone
  e. Testosterone

65. Spermatogenesis occurs in the

  a. Prostate gland
  b. Vas deferens
  c. Seminal vesicles
  d. Penis
  e. Seminiferous tubules

66. In which of the following stages of embryo development are the three primary germ layers first present?

  a. Zygote
  b. Gastrula
  c. Morula
  c. Blastula
  e. Coelomate

Copyright © Mometrix Media. You have been licensed one copy of this document for personal use only. Any other reproduction or redistribution is strictly prohibited. All rights reserved.

67. Which of the following extraembryonic membranes is an important source of nutrition in many non-human animal species but NOT in humans?

    a. Amnion
    b. Allantois
    c. Yolk sac
    d. Chorion
    e. Placenta

68. Which of the following is not a mechanism that contributes to cell differentiation and development in embryos?

    a. Asymmetrical cell division
    b. Asymmetrical cytoplasm distribution
    c. Organizer cells
    d. Location of cells on the lineage map
    e. Homeotic genes

69. Which of the following is true of the gastrula?

    a. It is a solid ball of cells
    b. It has three germ layers
    c. It is an extraembryonic membrane
    d. It gives rise to the blastula
    e. It derives from the zona pellucida

70. In birds, gastrulation occurs along the

    a. Dorsal lip of the embryo
    b. Embryonic disc
    c. Primitive streak
    d. Circular blastopore
    e. Inner cell mass

71. In snapdragons, the red (R) allele is incompletely dominant to the white (r) allele. If you saw a pink snapdragon, you would know

    a. Its phenotypes for both parents
    b. Its genotypes for both parents
    c. Its genotype for one parent
    d. Its genotype
    e. Its phenotype but not its genotype

72. In peas, purple flower color (P) is dominant to white (p) and tall stature (T) is dominant to dwarf (t). If the genes are unlinked, how many tall plants will be purple in the progeny of a $PpTt$ x $PpTT$ cross?

    a. 0
    b. ¼
    c. ½
    d. ¾
    e. 1

Copyright © Mometrix Media. You have been licensed one copy of this document for personal use only. Any other reproduction or redistribution is strictly prohibited. All rights reserved.

73. Which of the following does not obey the law of independent assortment?

    a. Two genes on opposite ends of a chromosome
    b. Flower color and height in snapdragons
    c. Two genes on separate chromosomes
    d. Seed color and flower color in peas
    e. Two genes next to each other on a chromosome

74. In a dihybrid cross between bean plants with red (R) wrinkled (w) seeds and white (r) smooth (W) seeds, the F1 progeny is all red and smooth. If the F1 plants are selfed, what proportion of the F2 will also be red and smooth if the genes are linked?

    a. All of them
    b. ¼
    c. 1/2
    d. 9/16
    e. None of them

75. Red-green color blindness is an X-linked trait. What is the probability that a mother that is heterozygous for this trait and a father with this trait will have affected children?

    a. 0
    b. ¼
    c. ½
    d. ¾
    e. 1

76. An individual with an AB blood type needs a blood transfusion. Which of the following types could NOT be a donor?

    a. O
    b. AB
    c. A
    d. B
    e. All of the above types can be donors

77. In humans, more than one gene contributes to the trait of hair color. This is an example of

    a. Pleiotropy
    b. Polygenic inheritance
    c. Codominance
    d. Linkage
    e. Epistasis

78. A child is born with type A blood and his mother has type A. Which of the following is NOT a possible combination of genotypes for the mother and father?

    a. IAIB and ii
    b. IAi and ii
    c. IA i and IB i
    d. IAi and IBIB
    e. IAIB and IBi

- 130 -

Copyright © Mometrix Media. You have been licensed one copy of this document for personal use only. Any other reproduction or redistribution is strictly prohibited. All rights reserved.

Population Biology

79. On a standard biomass pyramid, level 3 corresponds to which trophic level?
    a. Producers
    b. Decomposers
    c. Primary consumers
    d. Primary carnivores
    e. Secondary carnivores

80. In the food chain below, vultures represent

    grass → cow → wolf → vulture

    a. Scavengers
    b. Detritivores
    c. Primary carnivores
    d. Herbivores
    e. Secondary consumers

81. Which of the following is the major way in which carbon is released into the environment?
    a. Transpiration
    b. Respiration
    c. Fixation
    d. Sedimentation
    e. Absorption

82. What is the largest reservoir of nitrogen on the planet?
    a. The ocean
    b. Plants
    c. Soil
    d. The atmosphere
    e. Sediments, including fossil fuels

Copyright © Mometrix Media. You have been licensed one copy of this document for personal use only. Any other reproduction or redistribution is strictly prohibited. All rights reserved.

83. The diagram below represents the three types of survivorship curves, describing how mortality varies as species age. Which of the following species is most likely to exhibit Type I survivorship?

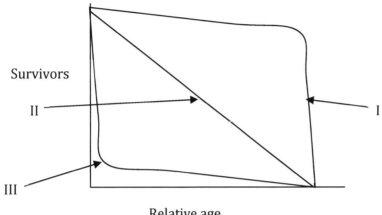

a. Frogs
b. Oysters
c. Salmon
d. Dolphins
e. Shrimp

84. A population of 1000 individuals has 110 births and 10 deaths in a year. Its growth rate (r) is equal to

a. 0.01 per year
b. 0.1 per year
c. 0.09 per year
d. 0.11 per year
e. 0.009 per year

85. During primary succession, which species would most likely be a pioneer species?

a. Lichens
b. Fir trees
c. Mosquitoes
d. Dragonflies
e. Mushrooms

86. Which of the following habitats would provide an opportunity for secondary succession?

a. A retreating glacier
b. Burned cropland
c. A newly formed volcanic island
d. A 500 year old forest
e. A sand dune

Copyright © Mometrix Media. You have been licensed one copy of this document for personal use only. Any other reproduction or redistribution is strictly prohibited. All rights reserved.

87. Which biome is most likely to support the growth of epiphytes?

    a. Deserts
    b. Tropical rain forests
    c. Temperate deciduous forests
    d. Taigas
    e. Savannas

88. Which of the following is NOT a natural dispersal process that would lead to species colonization on an island?

    a. Mussels carried into a lake on the hull of a ship
    b. Drought connecting an island to other land
    c. Floating seeds
    d. Animals swimming long distances
    e. Birds adapted to flying long distances

89. When a population reaches its carrying capacity

    a. Other populations will be forced out of the habitat
    b. Density-dependent factors no longer play a role
    c. Density-independent factors no longer play a role
    d. The population growth rate approaches zero
    e. The population size begins to decrease

90. Which of the following is an example of a density-dependent limiting factor?

    a. Air pollution by a factory
    b. The toxic effect of waste products
    c. Nearby volcanic eruptions
    d. Frosts
    e. Fires

91. Two species of finches are able to utilize the same food supply, but their beaks are different. They are able to coexist on an island because of

    a. Niche overlap
    b. Character displacement
    c. Resource partitioning
    d. Competitive exclusion
    e. Realized niches

92. Lichens consist of fungi and algae. The algae supply sugars through performing photosynthesis while the fungi provide minerals and a place to attach. This is an example of

    a. Mutualism
    b. Commensalism
    c. Parasitism
    d. Coevolution
    e. Resource partitioning

Copyright © Mometrix Media. You have been licensed one copy of this document for personal use only. Any other reproduction or redistribution is strictly prohibited. All rights reserved.

93. Which of the following of Lamarck's evolutionary ideas turned out to be true?

    a. Natural selection
    b. Organisms naturally transform into increasingly complex organisms
    c. Inheritance of acquired characters
    d. Body parts develop with increased usage and weaken with disuse
    e. Genes are the basic units of inheritance

94. The weight of adult wolves is within a fairly narrow range, even if they are well-fed in zoos. This is an example of

    a. Stabilizing selection
    b. Directional selection
    c. Disruptive selection
    d. Sexual selection
    e. Artificial selection

95. Which of the following is a trait that results from disruptive selection?

    a. Insecticide resistance
    b. Male peacocks have colorful plumage while females do not
    c. Within the same species, some birds have large bills, while others have small bills.
    d. Human height
    e. Different varieties of wheat

96. Which of the following conditions would promote evolutionary change?

    a. Neutral selection
    b. Random mating
    c. A large population
    d. An isolated population
    e. Gene flow

97. Which of the following would create the greatest amount of genetic variation for a diploid species in a single generation?

    a. Crossing over
    b. Mutation
    c. Hybridization
    d. Independent assortment of homologs
    e. Random joining of gametes

98. A population of pea plants has 25% dwarf plants and 75% tall plants. The tall allele, T is dominant to the dwarf allele, t. What is the frequency of the T allele?

    a. 0.75
    b. 0.67
    c. 0.5
    d. 0.25
    e. 0.16

Copyright © Mometrix Media. You have been licensed one copy of this document for personal use only. Any other reproduction or redistribution is strictly prohibited. All rights reserved.

99. Darwin's idea that evolution occurs by the gradual accumulation of small changes can be summarized as

    a. Punctuated equilibrium
    b. Phyletic gradualism
    c. Convergent evolution
    d. Adaptive radiation
    e. Sympatric speciation

100. Which of the following processes of speciation would most likely occur if a species of bird were introduced into a group of islands that were previously uninhabited by animals?

    a. Allopatric speciation
    b. Adaptive radiation
    c. Sympatric speciation
    d. Artificial speciation
    e. Hybridizing speciation

101. Hummingbirds drink nectar from *Ipomopsis* flowers. *Ipomopsis* are trumpet-shaped, and hummingbirds have long narrow beaks to access the nectar. These adaptations could best be described as

    a. Divergent evolution
    b. Convergent evolution
    c. Parallel evolution
    d. Coevolution
    e. Macroevolution

102. All of the following are homologous structures EXCEPT

    a. Bird feathers
    b. Elephant eyelashes
    c. Human fingernails
    d. Dog fur
    e. Insect exoskeleton

103. Human predation has cause the population of cheetahs to decline dramatically. Changes in allele frequencies in the remaining population of cheetahs would most likely be due to

    a. Mutation
    b. The bottleneck effect
    c. The founder effect
    d. Gene flow
    e. Natural selection

104. The first living cells on earth were most likely

    a. Heterotrophs
    b. Autotrophs
    c. Aerobic
    d. Eukaryotes
    e. Photosynthetic

Copyright © Mometrix Media. You have been licensed one copy of this document for personal use only. Any other reproduction or redistribution is strictly prohibited. All rights reserved.

105. Evidence that humans share a common ancestor with other primates includes all of the following EXCEPT

    a. DNA sequence
    b. Fossil evidence of intermediate species
    c. Analogous structures
    d. Homologous structures
    e. Radiometric dating of fossils

For questions 106 – 108, match the sentence(s) with the choice below that most closely matches it. Each lettered choice may be used more than once or not at all.

    a. Associative learning
    b. Imprinting
    c. Habituation
    d. Chemical communication
    e. Territoriality

106. Sea anemones pull food into their mouths by withdrawing their tentacles. If the tentacles are stimulated with a non-food item, they will ignore the stimulus after a few futile attempts to capture the food.

107. Queen bees secrete pheromones that are eaten by workers and prevent the workers from being able to reproduce.

108. Salmon hatch in freshwater streams and then migrate to the ocean to mature. When they are mature, they swim upstream to their birthplace to spawn.

109. The species *Homo sapiens* first appeared in the fossil record approximately

    a. 10 million years ago
    b. 1 million years ago
    c. 100,000 years ago
    d. 10,000 years ago
    e. 6,000 years ago

110. Which of the following demographic changes would lead to a population with an older age composition?

    a. Increased birth rate
    b. Environmental pollution
    c. Increased availability of food
    d. Medical advancements that increase life expectancy
    e. Introduction of contraceptives

111. Which of the following factors has the greatest impact on birth rate in humans?

    a. The carrying capacity of the earth
    b. Age at reproductive maturity
    c. Reproductive lifetime
    d. Survivorship of offspring to reproductive maturity
    e. Socioeconomic factors

Copyright © Mometrix Media. You have been licensed one copy of this document for personal use only. Any other reproduction or redistribution is strictly prohibited. All rights reserved.

112. Which of the following organisms would be most likely to have mercury in their bodies?

    a. Mosquitoes
    b. Carnivorous insects
    c. Frogs
    d. Filter-feeding fish
    e. Fish-eating birds

113. Clear-cutting of rain forests leads to all of the following consequences EXCEPT

    a. Climate change
    b. Erosion
    c. Reduction in species diversity
    d. Air pollution
    e. Desertification

114. Burning fossil fuels releases sulfur dioxide and nitrogen dioxide. These pollutants lead to which environmental problem?

    a. Denitrification
    b. Acid rain
    c. Global climate change
    d. Ozone depletion
    e. Eutrophication

115. Genetic engineering

    a. Is a form of human reproduction
    b. Involves introducing new proteins to a cell
    c. Involves transient expression of genes
    d. Can have no environmental affects
    e. Requires using restriction enzymes to cut DNA

Copyright © Mometrix Media. You have been licensed one copy of this document for personal use only. Any other reproduction or redistribution is strictly prohibited. All rights reserved.

Answers and Explanations

Molecular and Cellular Biology

1. C: The hydrogen bonds between water molecules cause water molecules to attract each other (negative pole to positive pole. and "stick" together. This gives water a high surface tension, which allows small living organisms, such as water striders, to move across its surface. Since water is a polar molecule, it readily dissolves other polar and ionic molecules such as carbohydrates and amino acids. Polarity alone is not sufficient to make something soluble in water, however; for example, cellulose is polar but its molecular weight is so large that it is not soluble in water.

2. D: An exothermic reaction releases energy, whereas an endothermic reaction requires energy. The breakdown of a chemical compound is an example of a decomposition reaction (AB → A + B.. A combination reaction (A + B →AB. is the reverse of a decomposition reaction, and a replacement (displacement) reaction is one where compound breaks apart and forms a new compound plus a free reactant (AB + C →AC + B or AB + CD → AD + CB.

3. B: Glycogen is a polysaccharide, a molecule composed of many bonded glucose molecules. Glucose is a carbohydrate, and all carbohydrates are composed of only carbon, oxygen, and hydrogen. Most other metabolic compounds contain other atoms, particularly nitrogen, phosphorous, and sulfur.

4. A: Long term energy storage in animals takes the form of fat. Animals also store energy as glycogen, and plants store energy as starch. , but these substances are for shorter-term use. Fats are a good storage form for chemical energy because fatty acids bond to glycerol in a condensation reaction to form fats (triglycerides). This reaction, which releases water, allows for the compacting of high-energy fatty acids in a concentrated form.

5. B: Some RNA molecules in extant organisms have enzymatic activity; for example the formation of peptide bonds on ribosomes is catalyzed by an RNA molecule. This and other information has led scientists to believe that the most likely molecules to first demonstrate enzymatic activity were RNA molecules.

6. E: Endocytosis is a process by which cells absorb larger molecules or even tiny organisms, such as bacteria, than would be able to pass through the plasma membrane. Endocytic vesicles containing molecules from the extracellular environment often undergo further processing once they enter the cell.

7. C: Chloroplasts contain the light-absorbing compound chlorophyll, which is essential in photosynthesis. This gives leaves their green color. Chloroplasts also contain yellow and red carotenoid pigments, which give leaves red and yellow colors in the fall as chloroplasts lose their chlorophyll.

8. A: Osmosis is the movement of water molecules (not solutes) across a semi-permeable membrane. Water moves from a region of higher concentration to a region of lower concentration. Osmosis occurs when the concentrations of a solute differ on either side of a semi-permeable membrane. For example, a cell (containing a higher concentration of water) in a salty solution (containing a lower concentration of water) will lose water as water leaves the cell. This continues until the solution outside the cell has the same salt concentration as the cytoplasm.

- 138 -

Copyright © Mometrix Media. You have been licensed one copy of this document for personal use only. Any other reproduction or redistribution is strictly prohibited. All rights reserved.

9. D: Both prokaryotes and eukaryotes interact with the extracellular environment and use membrane-bound or membrane-associated proteins to achieve this. They both use diffusion and active transport to move materials in and out of their cells. Prokaryotes have very few proteins associated with their DNA, whereas eukaryotes' DNA is richly studded with proteins. Both types of living things can have flagella, although with different structural characteristics in the two groups. The most important differences between prokaryotes and eukaryotes are the lack of a nucleus and membrane-bound organelles in prokaryotes.

10. B: Bacteria and cyanobacteria have cell walls constructed from peptidoglycans – a polysaccharide and protein molecule. Other types of organisms with cell walls, for instance, plants and fungi, have cell walls composed of different polysaccharides. Plant cell walls are composed of cellulose, and fungal cell walls are composed of chitin.

11. D: Enzymes act as catalysts for biochemical reactions. A catalyst is not consumed in a reaction, but, rather, lowers the activation energy for that reaction. The potential energy of the substrate and the product remain the same, but the activation energy—the energy needed to make the reaction progress—can be lowered with the help of an enzyme.

12. A: A cofactor is an inorganic substance that is required for an enzymatic reaction to occur. Cofactors bind to the active site of the enzyme and enable the substrate to fit properly. Many cofactors are metal ions, such as zinc, iron, and copper.

13. D: Enzyme inhibitors attach to an enzyme and block substrates from entering the active site, thereby preventing enzyme activity. As stated in the question, cyanide is a poison that irreversibly binds to an enzyme and blocks its active site, thus fitting the definition of an enzyme inhibitor.

14. A: Because the energy of the products is less than the energy of the substrate, the reaction releases energy and is an exergonic reaction.

15. D: Enzymes are substrate-specific. Most enzymes catalyze only one biochemical reaction. Their active sites are specific for a certain type of substrate and do not bind to other substrates and catalyze other reactions.

16. C: Lactic acid fermentation converts pyruvate into lactate using high-energy electrons from NADH. This process allows ATP production to continue in anaerobic conditions by providing NAD^+ so that ATP can be made in glycolysis.

17. B: Proteins in the inner membrane of the mitochondrion accept high-energy electrons from NAD and $FADH_2$, and in turn transport protons from the matrix to the intermembrane space. The high proton concentration in the intermembrane space creates a gradient which is harnessed by ATP synthase to produce ATP.

18. E: Electrons trapped by the chlorophyll P680 molecule in photosystem II are energized by light. They are then transferred to electron acceptors in an electron transport chain.

19. D: CAM photosynthesis occurs in plants that grow where water loss must be minimized, such as cacti. These plants open their stomata and fix CO_2 at night. During the day, stomata are closed, reducing water loss. Thus, photosynthesis can proceed without water loss.

20. B: DNA wrapped around histone proteins is called chromatin. In a eukaryotic cell, DNA is always associated with protein; it is not "naked" as with prokaryotic cells.

Copyright © Mometrix Media. You have been licensed one copy of this document for personal use only. Any other reproduction or redistribution is strictly prohibited. All rights reserved.

21. C: The diploid chromosome number for humans is 46. After DNA duplication but before the first cell division of meiosis, there are 92 chromatids (46 chromosomes). After meiosis I is completed, the chromosome number is halved and equals 23. Each daughter cell is haploid, but the chromosomes are still paired (sister chromatids). During meiosis II, the two sister chromatids of each chromosome separate, resulting in 23 haploid chromosomes per germ cell.

22. D: In anaphase I, homologous chromosome pairs segregate randomly into daughter cells. This means that each daughter cell contains a unique combination of chromosomes that is different from the mother cell and different from its cognate daughter cell.

23. C: Although there are two cell divisions in meiosis, DNA replication occurs only once. It occurs in interphase I, before M phase begins.

24. B: The synaptonemal complex is the point of contact between homologous chromatids. It is formed when nonsister chromatids exchange genetic material through crossing over. Once prophase of meiosis I has completed, crossovers have resolved and the synaptonemal complex no longer exists. Rather, sister chromatids are held together at their centromeres prior to separation in anaphase II.

25. C: Genes code for proteins, and genes are discrete lengths of DNA on chromosomes. An allele is a variant of a gene (different DNA sequence.. In diploid organisms, there may be two versions of each gene.

26. D: The enzyme helicase unwinds DNA. It depends on several other proteins to make the unwinding run smoothly, however. Single-strand binding protein holds the single stranded DNA in place, and topoisomerase helps relieve tension at the replication fork.

27. D: DNA is composed of nucleotides joined together in long chains. Nucleotides are composed of a pentose sugar, a phosphate group, and a nitrogenous base. The bases form the "rungs" of the ladder at the core of the DNA helix and the pentose-phosphates are on its outside, or backbone.

28. B: DNA replication begins with a short segment of RNA (not DNA.. DNA polymerase cannot begin adding nucleotides without an existing piece of DNA (a primer).

29. A: DNA synthesis on the lagging strand forms short segments called Okazaki fragments. Because DNA polymerase can only add nucleotides in the $5' \rightarrow 3'$ direction, lagging strand synthesis is discontinuous. The final product is formed when DNA ligase joins Okazaki fragments together.

30. D: Each time a cell divides; a few base pairs of DNA at the end of each chromosome are lost. Telomerase is an enzyme that uses a built-in template to add a short sequence of DNA over and over at the end of chromosomes—a sort of protective "cap". This prevents the loss of genetic material with each round of DNA replication.

31. D: DNA polymerase does not match base pairs with 100% fidelity. Some level of mismatching is present for all DNA polymerases, and this is a source of mutation in nature. Cells have mechanisms of correcting base pair mismatches, but they do not fix all of them.

32. C: Insertions and deletions cause frameshift mutations. These mutations cause all subsequent nucleotides to be displaced by one position, and thereby cause all the amino acids to be different than they would have been if the mutation had not occurred.

- 140 -

Copyright © Mometrix Media. You have been licensed one copy of this document for personal use only. Any other reproduction or redistribution is strictly prohibited. All rights reserved.

33. A: Transcription is the process of creating an RNA strand from a DNA template. All forms of RNA, for example mRNA, tRNA, and rRNA, are products of transcription.

34. C: The *lac* operon controls transcription of the gene that allows bacteria to metabolize lactose. It codes for both structural and regulatory proteins and includes promoter and operator sequences.

35. E: Operons are common to prokaryotes. They are units of DNA that control the transcription of DNA and code for their own regulatory proteins as well as structural proteins.

36. D: Conjugation is direct transfer of plasmid DNA between bacteria through a pilus. The F plasmid contains genes that enable bacteria to produce pili and is often the DNA that is transferred between bacteria.

37. D: In the lysogenic cycle, viral DNA gets incorporated into the DNA of the host. A virus in this dormant stage is called a provirus. Eventually, an external cue may trigger the virus to excise itself and begin the lytic cycle.

38. B: In the lytic cycle, viruses use host resources to produce viral DNA and proteins in order to create new viruses. They destroy the host cell in the process by lysing it. For this reason, actively replicating viruses are said to be in the lytic cycle.

39. C: Plasmids are small circular pieces of DNA found in bacteria that are widely used in recombinant DNA technology. They are cut with restriction enzymes and DNA of interest is ligated to them. They can then easily be used to transform bacteria.

Organismal Biology

40. D: The ovary houses the ovules in a flower. Pollen grains fertilize ovules to create seeds, and the ovary matures into a fruit.

41. C: Gymnosperms reproduce by producing pollen and ovules, but they do not have flowers. Instead, their reproductive structures are cones or cone-like structures.

42. E: Stomata are openings on leaves that allow for gas exchange, which is essential for photosynthesis. Stomata are formed by guard cells, which open and close based on their turgidity.

43. A: Monocots differ from dicots in that they have one cotyledon, or embryonic leaf in their embryos. They also have parallel veination, fibrous roots, petals in multiples of three, and a random arrangement of vascular bundles in their stems.

44. E: Nonvascular plants do not produce fruits like angiosperms and gymnosperms do. They generally reproduce sexually, but produce spores instead of seeds.

45. C: Angiosperms produce flowers, with ovules inside of ovaries. The ovaries become a fruit, with seeds inside. Gymnosperms have naked seeds that are produced in cones or cone like structures.

46. 76. A: The central, supporting pillar of the tree is known as heartwood. Heartwood does not function in the transport of water, and even though it is dead it will not decay or lose strength as long as the outer layers remain intact.

47. D: The phloem is the pipeline through which carbohydrates are transported to the roots. It is located outside of the xylem and lives for only a short time before becoming part of the outer bark.

Copyright © Mometrix Media. You have been licensed one copy of this document for personal use only. Any other reproduction or redistribution is strictly prohibited. All rights reserved.

48. B: In ferns, the mature diploid plant is called a sporophyte. Sporophytes undergo meiosis to produce spores, which develop into gametophytes, which produce gametes.

49. C: Alternation of generations means the alternation between the diploid and haploid phases in plants.

50. B: Anthers produce microspores (the male gametophytes of flowering plants), which undergo meiosis to produce pollen grains.

51. C: In flowering plants, the anthers house the male gametophytes (which produce sperm) and the pistils house the female gametophytes (which produce eggs). Eggs and sperm are haploid. All other tissues are solely diploid.

52. A: The plant hormone ethylene is responsible for fruit ripening. Auxins are involved in a range of processes involving growth and development.

53. C: Cytokinins stimulate cell division (cytokinesis) and have been found to delay senescence (aging). They are often sprayed on cut flowers and fruit to prolong their shelf life.

54. C: Day-neutral plants are not affected by day length in their flowering times. Rather, they respond to other environmental cues like temperature and water.

55. C: Plants exchange gases with the environment through pores in their leaves called stomata. Animals exchange gases with the environment in many different ways: small animals like flatworms exchange gases through their skin; insects use tracheae; and many species use lungs.

56. B: Platelets are cell fragments that are involved in blood clotting. Platelets are the site for the blood coagulation cascade. Its final steps are the formation of fibrinogen which, when cleaved, forms fibrin, the "skeleton" of the blood clot.

57. A: The large intestine's main function is the reabsorption of water into the body to form solid waste. It also allows for the absorption of vitamin K produced by microbes living inside the large intestine.

58. D: When Ca^{2+} channels open, calcium enters the axon terminal and causes synaptic vesicles to release neurotransmitter into the synaptic cleft.

59. C: In a positive feedback loop, an action intensifies a chain of events that, in turn, intensify the conditions that caused the action beyond normal limits. Nursing stimulates lactation, which promotes nursing. Contractions during childbirth, psychological hysteria, and sexual orgasm are all examples of positive feedback.

60. D: Mammals often warm themselves by altering their metabolism. Shivering warms animals due to the heat generated by contractions in trunk muscles.

61. A: HCG is secreted by the trophoblast, part of the early embryo, following implantation in the uterus. GnRH (gonadotropin-releasing hormone. is secreted by the hypothalamus, while LH (luteinizing hormone. and FSH (follicle-stimulating hormone. are secreted by the pituitary gland. GnRH stimulates the production of LH and FSH. LH stimulates ovulation and the production of estrogen and progesterone by the ovary in females, and testosterone production in males. FSH stimulates maturation of the ovarian follicle and estrogen production in females and sperm production in males.

Copyright © Mometrix Media. You have been licensed one copy of this document for personal use only. Any other reproduction or redistribution is strictly prohibited. All rights reserved.

62. E: The placenta secretes progesterone and estrogen once a pregnancy is established. Early in pregnancy, the placenta secretes hCG.

63. C: In oogenesis, meiosis I produces a secondary oocyte and a polar body. Both the first polar body and the secondary oocyte undergo meiosis II. The secondary oocyte divides to produce the ovum and the second polar body.

64. D: Positive feedback from rising levels of estrogen in the menstrual cycle produces a sudden surge of luteinizing hormone (LH). This high level triggers ovulation.

65. E: The testes contain hundreds of seminiferous tubules for the production of sperm, or spermatogenesis. This requires 64-72 days. Leydig cells surround the seminiferous tubules and produce male sex hormones called androgens, the most important of which is testosterone. Semen is made in the seminal vesicles, prostate gland, and other glands. Sperm are transferred to the penis via the epididymis, where they become motile, and thence through the vas deferens.

66. B: The gastrula is formed from the blastocyst, which contains a bilayered embryonic disc. One layer of this disc's inner cell mass further subdivides into the epiblast and the hypoblast, resulting in the three primary germ layers (endoderm, mesoderm, ectoderm).

67. C: In birds and reptiles, the yolk sac contains the yolk, the main source of nutrients for the embryo. In humans, the yolk sac is empty and embryos receive nutrition through the placenta. However, the yolk sac forms part of the digestive system and is where the earliest blood cells and blood vessels are formed.

68. D: A lineage map describes the fates of cells in the early embryo: in other words, it tells which germ layer different cells will occupy. In some small organisms such as the nematode *Caenorhabditis elegans*, all of the adult cells can be traced back to the egg. A lineage map is not a mechanism of embryo development, but rather a tool for describing it.

69. B: The gastrula is the first three-layered stage of the embryo, containing ectoderm, mesoderm, and endoderm

70. C: In birds, the invagination of gastrulation occurs along a line called a primitive streak. Cells migrate to the primitive streak, and the embryo becomes elongated.

71. D: You would know the snapdragon has an *Rr* genotype, but you would not know whether its parents had an *Rr* genotype or a combination of Rr and *rr* or *RR* and *rr*.

72. D: All the plants will be tall, and flower color will assort independently of stature. In a *Pp* x *Pp* cross, ¾ of the progeny will be purple.

73. E: Two genes next to, or within a specified close distance of, each other, are said to be linked. Linked genes do not follow the law of independent assortment because they are too close together to be segregated from each other in meiosis.

74. C: If the genes are linked, there would be only two kinds of alleles produced by the F1 plants: *Rw* and *rW*. A Punnet square with these alleles reveals that half the progeny will have both an *R* and a *W* allele.

75. C: Half of the boys will receive the color-blind allele from the mother, and the other half will receive the normal one. All the girls will receive the color-blind allele from the father; half of them

- 143 -

Copyright © Mometrix Media. You have been licensed one copy of this document for personal use only. Any other reproduction or redistribution is strictly prohibited. All rights reserved.

will also get one from the mother, while the other half will get the normal one. Therefore, half the children will be colorblind.

76. E: An individual with AB blood is tolerant to both the A carbohydrate on red blood cells and the B carbohydrate as "self" and can therefore accept any of the 4 different blood types.

77. B: When more than one gene contributes to a trait, inheritance of that trait is said to be polygenic. This type of inheritance does not follow the rules of Mendelian genetics.

78. D: The parents in D could only have offspring with AB or B blood types, not the A blood type.

Population Biology

79. D: At the lowest trophic level are the producers, followed by primary consumers. Primary carnivores follow consumers, followed by secondary carnivores.

80 A: Vultures eat carrion, or dead animals, so they are considered scavengers. Detritivores are heterotrophs that eat decomposing organic matter such as leaf litter. They are usually small.

81. B: Carbon is released in the form of CO_2 through respiration, burning, and decomposition.

82. D: Most nitrogen is in the atmosphere in the form of N_2. In order for it to be used by living things, it must be fixed by nitrogen-fixing bacteria. These microorganisms convert N_2 to ammonia, which then forms NH_4^+ (ammonium).

83. D: Type I curves describe species in which most individuals survive to middle age, after which deaths increase. Dolphins have few offspring, provide extended care to the young, and live a long time.

84. B: The growth rate is equal to the difference between births and deaths divided by population size.

85. A: Pioneer species colonize vacant habitats, and the first such species in a habitat demonstrate primary succession. Succession on rock or lava often begins with lichens. Lichens need very little organic material and can erode rock into soil to provide a growth substrate for other organisms.

86. B: Secondary succession occurs when a habitat has been entirely or partially disturbed or destroyed by abandonment, burning, storms, etc.

87. B: Epiphytes are plants that grow in the canopy of trees, and the tropical rain forest has a rich canopy because of its density and extensive moisture.

88. A: Transportation by humans or human-associated means is not considered a natural dispersal process.

89. D: Within a habitat, there is a maximum number of individuals that can continue to thrive, known as the habitat's carrying capacity. When the population size approaches this number, population growth will stop.

90. B: Density-dependent limiting factors on population growth are factors that vary with population density. Pollution from a factory, volcanic eruptions, frosts, and fires do not vary as a function of population size. Waste products, however, increase with population density and could limit further population increases.

Copyright © Mometrix Media. You have been licensed one copy of this document for personal use only. Any other reproduction or redistribution is strictly prohibited. All rights reserved.

91. B: Character displacement means that, although similar, species in the same habitat have evolved characteristics that reduce competition between them. It occurs as a result of resource partitioning.

92. A: Because both species benefit, lichens constitute an example of mutualism.

93. D: Natural selection was Darwin's idea, not Lamarck's. Mendel discovered that genes are the basic units of inheritance. Lamarck's observation about use and disuse is true, although he did not connect it with the underlying mechanism of natural selection.

94. A: Stabilizing selection is a form of selection in which a particular trait, such as weight, becomes stable within a population. It results in reduced genetic variability, and the disappearance of alleles for extreme traits. Over time, the most common phenotypes survive.

95. C: Disruptive selection occurs when the environment favors alleles for extreme traits. In the example, seasonal changes can make different types of food available at different times of the year, favoring the large or short bills, respectively.

96. E: Options A-D all describe conditions that would lead to genetic equilibrium, where no evolution would occur. Gene flow, which is the introduction or removal of alleles from a population, would allow natural selection to work and could promote evolutionary change.

97. C: Hybridization between two different species would result in more genetic variation than sexual reproduction within a species.

98. C: According to Hardy-Weinberg equilibrium, $p + q = 1$ and $p^2 + 2pq + q^2 = 1$. In this scenario, $q^2 = 0.25$, so $q = 0.5$. p must also be 0.5.

99. B: Phyletic gradualism is the view that evolution occurs at a more or less constant rate. Contrary to this view, punctuated equilibrium holds that evolutionary history consists of long periods of stasis punctuated by geologically short periods of evolution. This theory predicts that there will be few fossils revealing intermediate stages of evolution, whereas phyletic gradualism views the lack of intermediate-stage fossils as a deficit in the fossil record that will resolve when enough specimens are collected.

100. B: Adaptive radiation is the evolution of several species from a single ancestor. It occurs when a species colonizes a new area and members diverge geographically as they adapt to somewhat different conditions.

101. D: In coevolution, one species responds to new adaptations in another. Coevolution occurs between predator and prey, pathogens and the immune systems of animals, and plants and their pollinators.

102 E: Structures are homologous because they derive from a common ancestor. Insects do not share a common ancestor with birds and mammals. Birds and mammals share a reptile ancestor.

103. B: The bottleneck effect occurs when populations undergo a dramatic decrease in size. It could be due to natural or artificial causes.

104. A: The first living organisms probably had not yet evolved the ability to synthesize their own organic molecules for food. They were probably heterotrophs that consumed nutrition from the "organic soup."

Copyright © Mometrix Media. You have been licensed one copy of this document for personal use only. Any other reproduction or redistribution is strictly prohibited. All rights reserved.

105. C: Analogous structures do not reveal anything about common ancestors between species. They are simply features that arise due to adapting to similar ecological conditions.

106. C: Habituation is a learned behavior that teaches an animal to ignore meaningless or neutral stimuli.

107. D: Pheromones are chemicals used by animals for communication. They are released by certain individuals and elicit behavioral changes in other individuals.

108. B: Imprinting is a program for acquiring a behavior if an appropriate stimulus is given during a critical time period early in life. Salmon are imprinted with the odors of their birthplace after hatching.

109. C: *Homo sapiens* are thought to have evolved in Africa approximately 100,000 years ago.

110. D: Prolonging the life of individuals in a current population will lead to an older age composition. An increased birth rate will cause population growth, but a greater proportion will be younger, not older.

111. E: With many species, factors like food, space, and predation have large effects on reproduction. Humans are able to control or at least affect many of these challenges, as well as the reproductive process itself, so other factors like education, religion, wealth, and access to health care are more significant factors in birth rates.

112. E: Mercury is a fat-soluble pollutant and can be stored in body tissues. Animals higher up the food chain that eat other animals are most likely to accumulate mercury in their bodies.

113. D: Air pollution would not be a direct result of clear-cutting forests. It would result in increased atmospheric CO_2, however, as well as localized climate change. Transpiration from trees in the tropical rain forest contributes largely to cloud formation and rain, so rainfall decreases because of clear-cutting, resulting in desertification.

114. B: When sulfur dioxide and nitrogen dioxide mix with water and other substances in the atmosphere, they produce sulfuric acid and nitric acid. These acids kill plants and animals when they reach the surface of the earth.

115. E: Genetic engineering is a general term to describe altering DNA sequences through adding or removing pieces of DNA from a native sequence. Restriction enzymes perform this "clipping" function.

Copyright © Mometrix Media. You have been licensed one copy of this document for personal use only. Any other reproduction or redistribution is strictly prohibited. All rights reserved.

How to Overcome Test Anxiety

Just the thought of taking a test is enough to make most people a little nervous. A test is an important event that can have a long-term impact on your future, so it's important to take it seriously and it's natural to feel anxious about performing well. But just because anxiety is normal, that doesn't mean that it's helpful in test taking, or that you should simply accept it as part of your life. Anxiety can have a variety of effects. These effects can be mild, like making you feel slightly nervous, or severe, like blocking your ability to focus or remember even a simple detail.

If you experience test anxiety—whether severe or mild—it's important to know how to beat it. To discover this, first you need to understand what causes test anxiety.

Causes of Test Anxiety

While we often think of anxiety as an uncontrollable emotional state, it can actually be caused by simple, practical things. One of the most common causes of test anxiety is that a person does not feel adequately prepared for their test. This feeling can be the result of many different issues such as poor study habits or lack of organization, but the most common culprit is time management. Starting to study too late, failing to organize your study time to cover all of the material, or being distracted while you study will mean that you're not well prepared for the test. This may lead to cramming the night before, which will cause you to be physically and mentally exhausted for the test. Poor time management also contributes to feelings of stress, fear, and hopelessness as you realize you are not well prepared but don't know what to do about it.

Other times, test anxiety is not related to your preparation for the test but comes from unresolved fear. This may be a past failure on a test, or poor performance on tests in general. It may come from comparing yourself to others who seem to be performing better or from the stress of living up to expectations. Anxiety may be driven by fears of the future—how failure on this test would affect your educational and career goals. These fears are often completely irrational, but they can still negatively impact your test performance.

> **Review Video:** 3 Reasons You Have Test Anxiety
> Visit mometrix.com/academy and enter code: 428468

Copyright © Mometrix Media. You have been licensed one copy of this document for personal use only. Any other reproduction or redistribution is strictly prohibited. All rights reserved.

Elements of Test Anxiety

As mentioned earlier, test anxiety is considered to be an emotional state, but it has physical and mental components as well. Sometimes you may not even realize that you are suffering from test anxiety until you notice the physical symptoms. These can include trembling hands, rapid heartbeat, sweating, nausea, and tense muscles. Extreme anxiety may lead to fainting or vomiting. Obviously, any of these symptoms can have a negative impact on testing. It is important to recognize them as soon as they begin to occur so that you can address the problem before it damages your performance.

> **Review Video: 3 Ways to Tell You Have Test Anxiety**
> Visit mometrix.com/academy and enter code: 927847

The mental components of test anxiety include trouble focusing and inability to remember learned information. During a test, your mind is on high alert, which can help you recall information and stay focused for an extended period of time. However, anxiety interferes with your mind's natural processes, causing you to blank out, even on the questions you know well. The strain of testing during anxiety makes it difficult to stay focused, especially on a test that may take several hours. Extreme anxiety can take a huge mental toll, making it difficult not only to recall test information but even to understand the test questions or pull your thoughts together.

> **Review Video: How Test Anxiety Affects Memory**
> Visit mometrix.com/academy and enter code: 609003

Effects of Test Anxiety

Test anxiety is like a disease—if left untreated, it will get progressively worse. Anxiety leads to poor performance, and this reinforces the feelings of fear and failure, which in turn lead to poor performances on subsequent tests. It can grow from a mild nervousness to a crippling condition. If allowed to progress, test anxiety can have a big impact on your schooling, and consequently on your future.

Test anxiety can spread to other parts of your life. Anxiety on tests can become anxiety in any stressful situation, and blanking on a test can turn into panicking in a job situation. But fortunately, you don't have to let anxiety rule your testing and determine your grades. There are a number of relatively simple steps you can take to move past anxiety and function normally on a test and in the rest of life.

> **Review Video: How Test Anxiety Impacts Your Grades**
> Visit mometrix.com/academy and enter code: 939819

Copyright © Mometrix Media. You have been licensed one copy of this document for personal use only. Any other reproduction or redistribution is strictly prohibited. All rights reserved.

Physical Steps for Beating Test Anxiety

While test anxiety is a serious problem, the good news is that it can be overcome. It doesn't have to control your ability to think and remember information. While it may take time, you can begin taking steps today to beat anxiety.

Just as your first hint that you may be struggling with anxiety comes from the physical symptoms, the first step to treating it is also physical. Rest is crucial for having a clear, strong mind. If you are tired, it is much easier to give in to anxiety. But if you establish good sleep habits, your body and mind will be ready to perform optimally, without the strain of exhaustion. Additionally, sleeping well helps you to retain information better, so you're more likely to recall the answers when you see the test questions.

Getting good sleep means more than going to bed on time. It's important to allow your brain time to relax. Take study breaks from time to time so it doesn't get overworked, and don't study right before bed. Take time to rest your mind before trying to rest your body, or you may find it difficult to fall asleep.

> **Review Video: The Importance of Sleep for Your Brain**
> Visit mometrix.com/academy and enter code: 319338

Along with sleep, other aspects of physical health are important in preparing for a test. Good nutrition is vital for good brain function. Sugary foods and drinks may give a burst of energy but this burst is followed by a crash, both physically and emotionally. Instead, fuel your body with protein and vitamin-rich foods.

Also, drink plenty of water. Dehydration can lead to headaches and exhaustion, especially if your brain is already under stress from the rigors of the test. Particularly if your test is a long one, drink water during the breaks. And if possible, take an energy-boosting snack to eat between sections.

> **Review Video: How Diet Can Affect your Mood**
> Visit mometrix.com/academy and enter code: 624317

Along with sleep and diet, a third important part of physical health is exercise. Maintaining a steady workout schedule is helpful, but even taking 5-minute study breaks to walk can help get your blood pumping faster and clear your head. Exercise also releases endorphins, which contribute to a positive feeling and can help combat test anxiety.

When you nurture your physical health, you are also contributing to your mental health. If your body is healthy, your mind is much more likely to be healthy as well. So take time to rest, nourish your body with healthy food and water, and get moving as much as possible. Taking these physical steps will make you stronger and more able to take the mental steps necessary to overcome test anxiety.

> **Review Video: How to Stay Healthy and Prevent Test Anxiety**
> Visit mometrix.com/academy and enter code: 877894

Copyright © Mometrix Media. You have been licensed one copy of this document for personal use only. Any other reproduction or redistribution is strictly prohibited. All rights reserved.

Mental Steps for Beating Test Anxiety

Working on the mental side of test anxiety can be more challenging, but as with the physical side, there are clear steps you can take to overcome it. As mentioned earlier, test anxiety often stems from lack of preparation, so the obvious solution is to prepare for the test. Effective studying may be the most important weapon you have for beating test anxiety, but you can and should employ several other mental tools to combat fear.

First, boost your confidence by reminding yourself of past success—tests or projects that you aced. If you're putting as much effort into preparing for this test as you did for those, there's no reason you should expect to fail here. Work hard to prepare; then trust your preparation.

Second, surround yourself with encouraging people. It can be helpful to find a study group, but be sure that the people you're around will encourage a positive attitude. If you spend time with others who are anxious or cynical, this will only contribute to your own anxiety. Look for others who are motivated to study hard from a desire to succeed, not from a fear of failure.

Third, reward yourself. A test is physically and mentally tiring, even without anxiety, and it can be helpful to have something to look forward to. Plan an activity following the test, regardless of the outcome, such as going to a movie or getting ice cream.

When you are taking the test, if you find yourself beginning to feel anxious, remind yourself that you know the material. Visualize successfully completing the test. Then take a few deep, relaxing breaths and return to it. Work through the questions carefully but with confidence, knowing that you are capable of succeeding.

Developing a healthy mental approach to test taking will also aid in other areas of life. Test anxiety affects more than just the actual test—it can be damaging to your mental health and even contribute to depression. It's important to beat test anxiety before it becomes a problem for more than testing.

> **Review Video: Test Anxiety and Depression**
> Visit mometrix.com/academy and enter code: 904704

Copyright © Mometrix Media. You have been licensed one copy of this document for personal use only. Any other reproduction or redistribution is strictly prohibited. All rights reserved.

Study Strategy

Being prepared for the test is necessary to combat anxiety, but what does being prepared look like? You may study for hours on end and still not feel prepared. What you need is a strategy for test prep. The next few pages outline our recommended steps to help you plan out and conquer the challenge of preparation.

Step 1: Scope Out the Test

Learn everything you can about the format (multiple choice, essay, etc.) and what will be on the test. Gather any study materials, course outlines, or sample exams that may be available. Not only will this help you to prepare, but knowing what to expect can help to alleviate test anxiety.

Step 2: Map Out the Material

Look through the textbook or study guide and make note of how many chapters or sections it has. Then divide these over the time you have. For example, if a book has 15 chapters and you have five days to study, you need to cover three chapters each day. Even better, if you have the time, leave an extra day at the end for overall review after you have gone through the material in depth.

If time is limited, you may need to prioritize the material. Look through it and make note of which sections you think you already have a good grasp on, and which need review. While you are studying, skim quickly through the familiar sections and take more time on the challenging parts. Write out your plan so you don't get lost as you go. Having a written plan also helps you feel more in control of the study, so anxiety is less likely to arise from feeling overwhelmed at the amount to cover. A sample plan may look like this:

- Day 1: Skim chapters 1–4, study chapter 5 (especially pages 31–33)
- Day 2: Study chapters 6–7, skim chapters 8–9
- Day 3: Skim chapter 10, study chapters 11–12 (especially pages 87–90)
- Day 4: Study chapters 13–15
- Day 5: Overall review (focus most on chapters 5, 6, and 12), take practice test

Step 3: Gather Your Tools

Decide what study method works best for you. Do you prefer to highlight in the book as you study and then go back over the highlighted portions? Or do you type out notes of the important information? Or is it helpful to make flashcards that you can carry with you? Assemble the pens, index cards, highlighters, post-it notes, and any other materials you may need so you won't be distracted by getting up to find things while you study.

If you're having a hard time retaining the information or organizing your notes, experiment with different methods. For example, try color-coding by subject with colored pens, highlighters, or post-it notes. If you learn better by hearing, try recording yourself reading your notes so you can listen while in the car, working out, or simply sitting at your desk. Ask a friend to quiz you from your flashcards, or try teaching someone the material to solidify it in your mind.

Step 4: Create Your Environment

It's important to avoid distractions while you study. This includes both the obvious distractions like visitors and the subtle distractions like an uncomfortable chair (or a too-comfortable couch that makes you want to fall asleep). Set up the best study environment possible: good lighting and a

Copyright © Mometrix Media. You have been licensed one copy of this document for personal use only. Any other reproduction or redistribution is strictly prohibited. All rights reserved.

comfortable work area. If background music helps you focus, you may want to turn it on, but otherwise keep the room quiet. If you are using a computer to take notes, be sure you don't have any other windows open, especially applications like social media, games, or anything else that could distract you. Silence your phone and turn off notifications. Be sure to keep water close by so you stay hydrated while you study (but avoid unhealthy drinks and snacks).

Also, take into account the best time of day to study. Are you freshest first thing in the morning? Try to set aside some time then to work through the material. Is your mind clearer in the afternoon or evening? Schedule your study session then. Another method is to study at the same time of day that you will take the test, so that your brain gets used to working on the material at that time and will be ready to focus at test time.

Step 5: Study!

Once you have done all the study preparation, it's time to settle into the actual studying. Sit down, take a few moments to settle your mind so you can focus, and begin to follow your study plan. Don't give in to distractions or let yourself procrastinate. This is your time to prepare so you'll be ready to fearlessly approach the test. Make the most of the time and stay focused.

Of course, you don't want to burn out. If you study too long you may find that you're not retaining the information very well. Take regular study breaks. For example, taking five minutes out of every hour to walk briskly, breathing deeply and swinging your arms, can help your mind stay fresh.

As you get to the end of each chapter or section, it's a good idea to do a quick review. Remind yourself of what you learned and work on any difficult parts. When you feel that you've mastered the material, move on to the next part. At the end of your study session, briefly skim through your notes again.

But while review is helpful, cramming last minute is NOT. If at all possible, work ahead so that you won't need to fit all your study into the last day. Cramming overloads your brain with more information than it can process and retain, and your tired mind may struggle to recall even previously learned information when it is overwhelmed with last-minute study. Also, the urgent nature of cramming and the stress placed on your brain contribute to anxiety. You'll be more likely to go to the test feeling unprepared and having trouble thinking clearly.

So don't cram, and don't stay up late before the test, even just to review your notes at a leisurely pace. Your brain needs rest more than it needs to go over the information again. In fact, plan to finish your studies by noon or early afternoon the day before the test. Give your brain the rest of the day to relax or focus on other things, and get a good night's sleep. Then you will be fresh for the test and better able to recall what you've studied.

Step 6: Take a practice test

Many courses offer sample tests, either online or in the study materials. This is an excellent resource to check whether you have mastered the material, as well as to prepare for the test format and environment.

Check the test format ahead of time: the number of questions, the type (multiple choice, free response, etc.), and the time limit. Then create a plan for working through them. For example, if you have 30 minutes to take a 60-question test, your limit is 30 seconds per question. Spend less time on the questions you know well so that you can take more time on the difficult ones.

Copyright © Mometrix Media. You have been licensed one copy of this document for personal use only. Any other reproduction or redistribution is strictly prohibited. All rights reserved.

If you have time to take several practice tests, take the first one open book, with no time limit. Work through the questions at your own pace and make sure you fully understand them. Gradually work up to taking a test under test conditions: sit at a desk with all study materials put away and set a timer. Pace yourself to make sure you finish the test with time to spare and go back to check your answers if you have time.

After each test, check your answers. On the questions you missed, be sure you understand why you missed them. Did you misread the question (tests can use tricky wording)? Did you forget the information? Or was it something you hadn't learned? Go back and study any shaky areas that the practice tests reveal.

Taking these tests not only helps with your grade, but also aids in combating test anxiety. If you're already used to the test conditions, you're less likely to worry about it, and working through tests until you're scoring well gives you a confidence boost. Go through the practice tests until you feel comfortable, and then you can go into the test knowing that you're ready for it.

Test Tips

On test day, you should be confident, knowing that you've prepared well and are ready to answer the questions. But aside from preparation, there are several test day strategies you can employ to maximize your performance.

First, as stated before, get a good night's sleep the night before the test (and for several nights before that, if possible). Go into the test with a fresh, alert mind rather than staying up late to study.

Try not to change too much about your normal routine on the day of the test. It's important to eat a nutritious breakfast, but if you normally don't eat breakfast at all, consider eating just a protein bar. If you're a coffee drinker, go ahead and have your normal coffee. Just make sure you time it so that the caffeine doesn't wear off right in the middle of your test. Avoid sugary beverages, and drink enough water to stay hydrated but not so much that you need a restroom break 10 minutes into the test. If your test isn't first thing in the morning, consider going for a walk or doing a light workout before the test to get your blood flowing.

Allow yourself enough time to get ready, and leave for the test with plenty of time to spare so you won't have the anxiety of scrambling to arrive in time. Another reason to be early is to select a good seat. It's helpful to sit away from doors and windows, which can be distracting. Find a good seat, get out your supplies, and settle your mind before the test begins.

When the test begins, start by going over the instructions carefully, even if you already know what to expect. Make sure you avoid any careless mistakes by following the directions.

Then begin working through the questions, pacing yourself as you've practiced. If you're not sure on an answer, don't spend too much time on it, and don't let it shake your confidence. Either skip it and come back later, or eliminate as many wrong answers as possible and guess among the remaining ones. Don't dwell on these questions as you continue—put them out of your mind and focus on what lies ahead.

Be sure to read all of the answer choices, even if you're sure the first one is the right answer. Sometimes you'll find a better one if you keep reading. But don't second-guess yourself if you do immediately know the answer. Your gut instinct is usually right. Don't let test anxiety rob you of the information you know.

Copyright © Mometrix Media. You have been licensed one copy of this document for personal use only. Any other reproduction or redistribution is strictly prohibited. All rights reserved.

If you have time at the end of the test (and if the test format allows), go back and review your answers. Be cautious about changing any, since your first instinct tends to be correct, but make sure you didn't misread any of the questions or accidentally mark the wrong answer choice. Look over any you skipped and make an educated guess.

At the end, leave the test feeling confident. You've done your best, so don't waste time worrying about your performance or wishing you could change anything. Instead, celebrate the successful completion of this test. And finally, use this test to learn how to deal with anxiety even better next time.

> **Review Video: 5 Tips to Beat Test Anxiety**
> Visit mometrix.com/academy and enter code: 570656

Important Qualification

Not all anxiety is created equal. If your test anxiety is causing major issues in your life beyond the classroom or testing center, or if you are experiencing troubling physical symptoms related to your anxiety, it may be a sign of a serious physiological or psychological condition. If this sounds like your situation, we strongly encourage you to seek professional help.

Copyright © Mometrix Media. You have been licensed one copy of this document for personal use only. Any other reproduction or redistribution is strictly prohibited. All rights reserved.

Thank You

We at Mometrix would like to extend our heartfelt thanks to you, our friend and patron, for allowing us to play a part in your journey. It is a privilege to serve people from all walks of life who are unified in their commitment to building the best future they can for themselves.

The preparation you devote to these important testing milestones may be the most valuable educational opportunity you have for making a real difference in your life. We encourage you to put your heart into it—that feeling of succeeding, overcoming, and yes, conquering will be well worth the hours you've invested.

We want to hear your story, your struggles and your successes, and if you see any opportunities for us to improve our materials so we can help others even more effectively in the future, please share that with us as well. **The team at Mometrix would be absolutely thrilled to hear from you!** So please, send us an email (support@mometrix.com) and let's stay in touch.

If you'd like some additional help, check out these other resources we offer for your exam:

http://MometrixFlashcards.com/NYSTCE

Copyright © Mometrix Media. You have been licensed one copy of this document for personal use only. Any other reproduction or redistribution is strictly prohibited. All rights reserved.

Additional Bonus Material

Due to our efforts to try to keep this book to a manageable length, we've created a link that will give you access to all of your additional bonus material.

Please visit http://www.mometrix.com/bonus948/nystcebiology to access the information.

Copyright © Mometrix Media. You have been licensed one copy of this document for personal use only. Any other reproduction or redistribution is strictly prohibited. All rights reserved.